DADA PERFORMANCE

DADA
PERFORMANCE

Edited by Mel Gordon

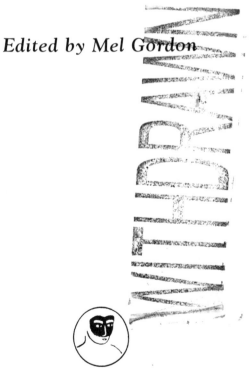

PAJ Publications
New York

TO JOSEPH AND ROSE GORDON

05 04 03 02 01 00 99 98 97 96   7 6 5 4 3

Distributed by The Johns Hopkins University Press
2715 North Charles Street
Baltimore, Maryland 21218-4319
The Johns Hopkins Press Ltd., London

Library of Congress Cataloging in Publication Data
Dada Performance
Library of Congress Catalog Card No.: 86-63184
ISBN: 1-55554-010-4 (cloth)
ISBN: 1-55554-011-2 (paper)

ACKNOWLEDGMENTS:
   Tristan Tzara's *Dada Manifesto* appeared in *Seven Dada Manifestos* by Tristan Tzara.
Copyright © 1977, 1981 by John Calder Publishers, Ltd. Reprinted by permission of Riverrun
Press, Inc.
   Tristan Tzara's *The First Celestial Adventure of Mr. Antipyrine, Fire Extinguisher*, transla-
tion by Ruth Wilson, appeared in *Yale/Theater*, vol. 4, no. 1, Winter 1972, pp. 133-141.
Reprinted by permission of the publisher.
   Ben Hecht's *Dadafest* appeared in *Letters from Bohemia* by Ben Hecht, Doubleday & Co.,
1964.
   Kurt Schwitters' *To All the Theatres of the World I Demand the MERZ Stage* appeared in
Art and the Stage, edited by Henning Rischbieter, Harry Abrams Publs., 1974. Reprinted by
permission of the publisher.
   André Breton and Philippe Soupault's *If You Please*, Acts 1-3, appeared in *Modern French
Theatre*, E. P. Dutton, 1964. Translation Copyright © 1964 by George E. Wellwarth.
Reprinted by permission of the publisher.
   André Breton and Philippe Soupault's *If You Please*, Act 4, by Annabelle Melzer, appeared
in *Latest Rage the Big Drum*, UMI Research Press, 1980. Reprinted by permission of the
publisher.
   Roger Vitrac's *Free Entry*, translation by Nahma Sandrow, appeared in *Surrealism*, Harper
and Row, 1972. Reprinted by permission of the publisher.
   These plays or descriptions of performances first appeared in *The Drama Review: Impressions of Africa, Berlin Dada Performance, The Mute Canary*, and *Handkerchief of Clouds*.

Design by Adam Parfrey

Printed in the United States of America on acid-free paper

Publication of this book has been made possible in part by grants received from the National
Endowment for the Arts, Washington, D.C., a federal agency, and the New York State Council on the Arts.

Contents

DaDa PERFORMANCE

An Introduction

Mel Gordon

The purity and absolutism of Dada created a fissure in the history of art. Not content to savage the schools and movements of the past like Futurism, Dada challenged the entire notion of art—even discounting its own productions. While the Dadas exhibited and staged creations and performances of all kinds, these were generally viewed as provocations, childish pranks, or the aesthetic critiques of madmen. The ghoulish humor and lack of seriousness confused the German and French art critics and historians of the World War I era. The vast documentation of the Dada movement, therefore, was created and preserved by its participants, not by its spectators and detractors. Ten years after Dada's demise in 1924, it was still viewed as a comical transition—or as a psychic slash-and-burn ploy—for its more successful cousin Surrealism. By the forties, however, there was a total reevaluation among the new generation of museum curators and art historians: Dada had finally received its separate and revolutionary status in twentieth-century art. In some ways it became the bedrock of all late modern and postmodern art.

In literary and theatre circles, Dada's fate has been less fortunate. Since its texts and performances were deliberately unintelligible, most scholars have ignored them completely. Even the handful of avant-garde drama historians have been uncertain of Dada's place in the history of performance. Do the Dadas deserve a paragraph in a guidebook to twentieth-century theatre, let alone a chapter? Should descriptions of their performances fall in sections on German-speaking or French theatre, or both? Dada performance texts, if they survive, seem to have little traditional value; the darkly humorous or frenzied side of Dada performance appears to fall outside the pale of serious academic reflection. (How can one, say, trace personal imagery in simultaneous poetry readings made up of nonsense syllables or chance-directed acting?) But if we measure a theatrical movement by its influence, rather than by the tastes of its critics or even by the after-thoughts of its participants, then the Dadas and their work become crucial in understanding the post-fifties avant-garde, especially in the phenomena of happenings, performance art, and Robert Wilson.

Dada's Prehistory

Bizarre or strange theatrics have filled Western performance history since before the time of Thespis. At the Theatron Dionysia, the Greek actor, Polus, needing inspiration for the role of Electra, carried on the cremated ashes of his son. Planned crucifixions of unsuspecting actors and live sexual intercourse were directorial techniques during the late Roman period that weaned spectators away from the comedies of Terence. Throughout the Renaissance, hundreds of patron-supported artists created astounding spectacles and unusual acting arenas that would seem avant-garde today. Guilio Camillo, for instance, designed a Kabbalistic stage of forty-nine boxes in 1524 that revealed all the secret wisdom of the world to his audiences. Perverse erotic enactments on fully-equipped proscenium stages in the private bordellos of eighteenth-century Vienna and Paris found wide support among the aristocracy, while court poets dourly spelled out Aristotle's rules to playwrights and censoring boards. In 1814, the German Romantic and follower of Franz Mesmer, Justinius Kerner built a puppet theatre, the Shadowgraph, that utilized the voices of real possessed persons while battery electricity encircled the seats of his twenty-four spectators.

The entire span of the nineteenth century was dotted with curious performance experiments but because of their occult, private, or sometimes illegal roots, few have found their way into the standard histories. Only the visionary Symbolists in France—and to a lesser degree in Russia—transformed their national drama repertories. Yet the avant-garde revolution that began with Symbolism in the 1890s merely changed what was mounted on the bourgeois stage, not how it was done. Symbolism's call for a cold, distant, dream-like style of acting with monotonous tones and choppy movements was met with critical laughter and little public attention. The dramas of Maurice Maeterlinck and other Symbolist playwrights fared much better when performed by famous actors in well-known theatres, complete with established composers and set designers.

Yet French Symbolism created a thirst for novelty and outrage in all the art forms. In 1896, the eccentric genius, Alfred Jarry, wrote the scandalous *Ubu Roi*, a post-Symbolist piece that many critics called the first modern play. Jarry's life and career bubbled with mad proto-Dada impulses. He lived in a room with five-foot ceilings; he ate all of his meals backwards and developed a new way of walking and speaking, stressing all of his syllables equally so his elocution resembled the patter of a machine-gun; he wore women's blouses and bicycle pantaloons; he invented the theory of Pataphysics, or the Science of Exceptions, which among other things proved the Immaculate Conception through simple calculus. Just before *Ubu*'s premiere, Jarry articulated a host of theatrical innovations, such as a handgrip by which each spectator could manipulate the stage action. But behind all of this was a curious passivity that was uncharacteristic of the later Dada movement.

Staged by Aurlien Lugné-Poe at the Théâtre de l'Oeuvre, *Ubu Roi* precipitated a genuine riot, but more than anything else it was the deliberate placement of obscenity and grotesque humor in a typical Parisian theatre setting that upset the middle-class spectators. Virtually none of Jarry's scenic inventions were used. Language, not the transformation of the proscenium relationship, brought the audience to its feet. In fact, Jarry's *Ubu*, however outrageous in thought, snugly fit into the shape and time frame of the boulevard comedy. Interestingly, totally dependent on the tastes of Lugné-Poe and other directors, Jarry could never again return to the stage. His black dramas were basically conceived in the mode of the time.

Raymond Roussel's *Impressions of Africa*, 1912

It is doubtful that Raymond Roussel (1877-1933) knew anything of *Ubu Roi*. More like a character from Jarry's imagination than Jarry himself, Roussel fulfills the chronicler's need for a Dada progenitor. Like the "Savage God" of the Théâtre de l'Oeuvre, Roussel was clearly an eccentric extraordinaire, but Roussel, born to wealth, had little need to compromise his aesthetic visions. Convinced that he would be more famous than Napoleon or Victor Hugo, Roussel traveled the world in a specially constructed trailer, which allowed him to completely shutter the windows, lest any imaginary rays emitted from his forehead or pen escape. Roussel's life and career resembled a human tapestry of the oddball phobias. One French psychoanalyst, Pierre Janet, found in Roussel a crucible of new and modern fears: the terror of dirtiness, of seeing women's breasts in public, of entering tunnels, of the slightest physical pain, of the interference of dressing and eating in his creative life, of violating the hidden order and arrangement of objects, to name a few.

Trained as a musician at the Conservatoire, Roussel despised the burgeoning naturalistic and realistic acting styles that engulfed the Parisian theatres of the 1890s. Instead, Roussel amused himself with melodramas, absurd operettas, and the French music hall. Roussel sometimes returned night after night to catch the small acting differences in a production. Other times, he would stare only at the theatre's sets and backdrops. Accompanied by a mistress—hired by Roussel's mother to cover for his homosexuality—and a little girl, Roussel frequented the Théâtre du Petit Monde and children's puppet shows. The drawings and lotteries at the conclusions of the children's productions thrilled Roussel, and whenever possible, he entered his mistress's name in them, always delighting when she won.

After his stockbroker father died in 1894, the seventeen-year-old Roussel developed a strange and complex language system based on multiple meanings of similarly spelled words. Using lipograms and metagrams that dropped certain letters from texts, interposing brackets and parentheses, and a half-dozen other invented linguistic mechanisms, Roussel created a neologistic lexicon that divorced language from everyday meaning. During a five-month creative hiatus in 1897, Roussel found an outlet for his kabbalistic techniques in the rhymed novel, *The Understudy*. Published at his own expense—as would all of Roussel's projects—*The Understudy* barely sold a few hundred copies, putting Roussel in a depressive state from which he never recovered. It finally occurred to him that he was not destined to become more famous than Napoleon or Richard Wagner.

Roussel continued to write his esoteric novels, which were quickly followed by critical rejection or indifference—much to Roussel's surprise and suffering. But in 1911, Roussel, at the joking suggestion of Edmond Rostand, decided to adapt *Impressions of Africa*, his melodramatic novel of "what has not been," for the French stage. By hiring some of the best known Parisian actors as well as a colorful and expensive publicity campaign—for instance, he bought the front cover of the performance journal *Le Théâtre*—Roussel felt the reviewers and public could not ignore his next genius production. And in a certain way, history proved him right.

After several false starts in 1911, *Impressions of Africa* was staged at the Théâtre Antoine from May 11 to June 10, 1912. Altogether some fifty-five performances were given in Paris and on tour during the summer in Northern France, Belgium and the Netherlands. The first two acts of *Impressions* provoked audiences by its sheer unintelligible detail about a party of Europeans shipwrecked on the West Africa coast. Only in the third act did Roussel's talent for the bizarre and "extra-retinal" appear. To ward off the killing effects of boredom in the tropics, the European cabaret artists create a contest of eight "Attractions," each more curious than the last. Using real freaks of nature, nightclub acts, and ingenious Rube Goldberg-like machinery, the third act both shocked and titillated its audience. Years later, Marcel Duchamp recalled, "It was magnificent. On the stage, there was a dummy and a snake that moved (or both moved?) a little bit. It was the absolute madness of the unusual." Apollinaire and Picabia were struck by Roussel's brave eccentricities too. Although Roussel mounted two more grotesque spectacles, *Locus Solus* (1922) and *The Star on the Forehead* (1924), only *Impressions of Africa* was so far ahead of its time; it inaugurated the spirit of Dada.

❧ Cabaret Voltaire Zurich, 1916-1919

The Dada revolution was born, promulgated, and nearly dissolved in Zurich at the Cabaret Voltaire. The product of a dozen highly-charged and contradictory characters, the Cabaret Voltaire and its artistic voice, Dada, matured in a textbook amoebic revolution: alternately expanding, contracting, doubling its leadership, and splitting into stronger and weaker spheres.

Why Zurich? To begin with, neutral Switzerland was an international magnet for political refugees and emigres in Central Europe even before 1914. Zurich's famed indifference to slightly-altered residence documentation mixed quiet, cat-petting revolutionaries like Vladimir Lenin (and his wife, Majestka Krupskaya) and Gregori Zinoviev with celebrated writers Frank Wedekind, Romain Rolland, Stefan Zweig, and James Joyce. Zurich also had a tradition for cabaret and variety entertainments. A curious, but boisterous, student population in Zurich's old quarter completed the complex equation.

Cabaret Voltaire begins with an unstable and somewhat mystic personality, Hugo Ball (1886-1927). Born near the French frontier in Germany, Ball studied philosophy at universities in Munich and Heidelberg. In 1910, he became involved with experimental theatre and cabaret. He even entered the acting program in Max Reinhardt's theatre school in Berlin, but quickly dropped out, spending much of his time with local Expressionist poets and playwrights. Like others of his generation, Ball's new theatrical vision became inflamed with Nietzschean vitalism, political Anarchism and Communism, and Vassily Kandinsky's call for an abstract *Gesamtkunstwerk*. At this time, Ball secured writing and directing contracts in the German theatre but few productions satisfied his avant-garde fancies. The cabaret and art-club soirees were closer to his occult visions. At a Dresden exhibit in 1913, he discovered Italian Futurism and dreamed of blending the emotionally-heightened and self-centered world of Expressionism with the mechanical assuredness of Futurism. (Ball was especially impressed that Marinetti handed out grenades, instead of cigars, at the birth of his son.)

The outbreak of war in September 1914 brought Ball immediately to the army recruiting office. Three times he was rejected due to heart problems but Ball needed an avenue to prove his Expressionist courage. In November he magically appeared on the Belgian front, hoping a loose rifle would fall into his hands. But what Ball saw during a two-week stay transformed his life: modern warfare—a faceless, body-shattering thud of artillery fire and poison gas cannisters. Now fearing that he would be soon inducted in his native Munich when he returned, Ball fled to Berlin. There he joined with Emmy Hennings (1885-1948), a notorious model, actress, chanteuse, cabaret dancer, modern poet, and accused forger.

For six months, Ball immersed himself in writing and philosophy. Hennings's skills in passport forgery brought them to Zurich under assumed names in May of 1915, but without working permits, they lived little better than vagabonds, sometimes rummaging through garbage bins and sleeping on the streets. Hennings, who had appeared in cheap roadside theatres and nightclubs throughout Germany and in Budapest and Moscow, was more accustomed to the itinerant performer's life than the scholarly Ball. Surviving on the fringes of Swiss society in league with tattooed ladies, gypsies, and side-show artists, Hemmings sang and Ball played piano in cabarets and variety halls. On the road, Ball become increasingly fascinated with drugs. His diary entries showed an embittered, almost suicidal train of thought. He no longer believed in the current materialist or idealist philosophies—be they Bolshevism or Expressionism. Ball was searching for something more real and absolute.

In January 1916, Ball met with Jan Ephraim, a retired Dutch sailor and owner of the Meierei, an inn in the center of Zurich's old city. Ball asked him for permission to start a nightclub. To his surprise, Ephraim agreed. A previous attempt by Swiss poets had failed but Ball's mad energy seemed to promise a hard-drinking and eating audience to fill the twenty or so tables. Quickly, word of mouth and press notices called for young artists and writers to contribute to the daily performances at the Cabaret Voltaire. For Ball, Voltaire represented reason incarnate, and his cabaret would go far beyond everyday, bourgeois logic to reach the gates of divine and life-giving reason.

While Ball and Hennings prepared for their opening performance on February 5, 1916, three Rumanians, an Alsatian, and an artist of unknown origin appeared at their door; these were Tristan Tzara (née Sami Rosenstock), the boundless and self-promoting propagandist of the soon-to-be international Dada revolution (1896-1963); Marcel Janco, a Futurist-influenced, architecture student from Bucharest; his brother, Georges; and Hans Arp, a modest and introverted modernist painter. The nucleus of Dada was forming.

That evening a chaotic mix of balalaika music, Wedekind poems, dance numbers, cabaret singing, recitations from Voltaire, and shouting in a kaleidoscopic environment of painting and prints by Janco, Marcel Slodki, Picasso, Arp, Marinetti word-drawings, and colored maps established the normal format of the Cabaret Voltaire. The lyrics of Verlaine and Mallarme and Futurist sound poems followed the next week with crazed piano-playing and anti-war diatribes.

By the end of the month Richard Huelsenbeck (1892-1974), a young German poet and friend of Ball arrived. Nearly complete, a self-satisfied feeling settled on the Cabaret Voltaire performers although allegiance of friendship—and therefore leadership—shifted constantly as personal bickering blended with artistic decisions. Ball referred his performers' play to the independent workings of a five-piece band (Ball, Huelsenbeck, Janco, Tzara, and Arp). His curious omission of Hennings's contribution is especially odd since newspaper critics praised her as the most accomplished performer of the bunch:

> The star of the cabaret, however, is Mrs. Emmy Hennings. Star of many nights of cabarets and poems. Years ago she stood by the rustling yellow curtain of a Berlin cabaret, hands on hips, as exuberant as a flowering shrub.
>
> *Züricher Post* (May 1916)

The first Cabaret Voltaire evenings were difficult to characterize. Despite provocative interludes and alcoholic audience feedback, they remained primarily literary ventures—with special programs devoted to Russian literature (including Chekhov), Jarry, and pseudo-African poetry. Only in March and April of 1916 did things radically change; for one, it found a name for its programmatic madness: Dada. Reportedly, the word Dada was selected at random from a French-German dictionary, where it was defined as French for "hobby-horse." (It seemed to have a multiplicity of meanings: "Yes, yes" in Russian; "Of course" in Rumanian; "Wet Nurse" in Italian; "Sister" in Swahili; and, according to Ball, "a sexually-obsessed cretin" in old Swabian slang.)

With a name, the naughty schoolboy's joke became a movement. The word Dada energized the group: manifestos and a magazine would soon accompany their specialized performances. Also, the word Dada gave shape to their art as well as their thinking. No longer were they imitators caught between German Expressionism and Italian Futurism; the Dadas were something quite different. Some early definitions: Ball, "Dada is a farce of nothingness in which all higher questions are involved; a gladiator's gesture, a play with shabby leftovers, the death warrant of posturing morality and abundance." (June 1916); Tzara, "Dada is our intensity; it erects inconsequential bayonets and the Sumatral head of German babies; Dada is life with neither bedroom slippers nor parallels; it is against and for unity and definitely against the future." (July 1916); Huelsenbeck, "Dada symbolizes the most primitive relation to the reality of the environment . . . Dada is a state of mind that can be revealed in any conversion . . . To be a Dada means to let oneself to be thrown by things, to oppose all sedimenta- tion . . . to be against this manifesto is to be a Dada" (April 1918).

The shape of Dada creation in painting, performance, and "word- artistry" moved more and more toward abstraction as its tone and content sharpened: now the Dadas declared war on all European culture—past, future, and present. Even the Italian Futurists had not gone so far with their love of warfare, machinery, and their own Futurist art. The Dadas attemp- ted to debunk the whole modernist notion of elite aesthetics, "Art falls asleep, Dada replaces it" or "Dada is produced in the mouth." To be sure, the Dadas shared Expressionism's sense of moral outrage and Futurism's ag- gressiveness but only Dada produced a vision of absolute negativity, of complete and willful derision against a world destroying itself.

The Cabaret Voltaire performances were never perceived as "theatre," and only occasionally counted as entertainment. The reading of manifestos overlapped with chansons, masked dances, lectures, and modern music. Ball, Huelsenbeck, and Tzara experimented with three kinds of poetic techniques: *Lautgedichte* (sound-poetry and noise-music); simultaneous poetry; and chance poetry. Although the Futurists and turn-of-the-century German poets had already pioneered the use of nonsense words and onomatopoetic sounds as literary devices, the Dadas incorporated them in- to moments of hysterical incantation with real drumbeats—when other per- formers were not imitating those sounds with their mouth. For Ball, the *Lautgedichte* were akin to wild episodes of glossolalia, the speaking in unknown or divine tongues; he called it religious verse without words. The recitation of words in various languages spoken at the same time, or simultaneous poetry, produced a strange comic effect that seemed ap- propriate for the multi-lingual Dadas. Literature was transforming itself in- to a game. Finally, chance poetry, Tzara's invention, was often created by randomly picking words out of a hat. Although interesting products resulted from Tzara's technique, the very idea of chance poetry spelled out an apocalyptic and revolutionizing message: anyone can make art.

The Zurich papers generally ignored the Cabaret Voltaire soirees. So the best descriptions, however impressionist, come from the diaries and memoirs of the Dadas themselves. Two 1916 examples from Arp and Tzara, respectively:

> In an overcrowded room, teeming with color, several fantastic per- sonages are seated on a platform; they are supposed to represent

Tzara, Janco, Ball, Mrs. Hennings, and your humble servant. We are in the midst of enormous tumult. The people about us shouting, laughing, gesticulating. We reply with sighs of love, salvos of hiccups, poetry, Wa Was, and the miowings of Medieval Bruitists. Janco plays an invisible violin and bows down to the ground. Mrs. Hennings, with the face of a madonna, tries to do the split. Huelsenbeck beats incessantly on his big drum while Ball, pale as a chalk dummy, accompanies him on the piano.

Jean Arp, *Dadaland*

In the presence of a compact crowd, Tzara demonstrates, we demand the right to piss in different colors. Huelsenbeck demonstrates, Ball demonstrates . . . the dogs bay and the dissection of Panama on the piano . . . shouted Poem—shouting and fighting in the hall, first row approves, second row declares itself incompetent, the rest shout, who is the strongest. The big drum is brought in, Huelsenbeck against 2000, *Ho osenlatz?* accentuated by the very big drum and little bells on his left foot and the people protest, shout, smash windowpanes, kill each other, demolish, fight, here come the police, interruption.

Tristan Tzara, *Dada* no. 4-5

As the stage antics and provocations grew to meet the Zurich schoolboys' expectations, Ball became disenchanted with Tzara's expanding role. Even Ephraim, the Meierei's owner, tired of the Dadas' recklessness, especially since they sometimes forgot to collect admissions and allowed drunken spectators to wreck his furniture. Moving to the Waag Hall on July 14, 1916, the Dadas staged a composite of their work. ("Music. Dance. Theory. Manifestos. Poetry. Paintings. Costumes. Masks.") Overly concerned with the famous spectators in the audience, Ball, unintentionally, went into a state of possession and had to be carried on the stage. Costumed as a kind of dervish-bird, Ball began to flap his wings as he read his *Lautgedichte*. Out of nowhere, he decided to recite his vowel and sound poetry in earnest, in the style of the Catholic liturgy.

For a moment I seemed to see, behind the Cubist mask, the pale anguished face of the ten-year-old boy who, at the parish requiems and high masses, had hung on the priest's every word, avid and trembling. Then the electric lights went out as arranged, and, bathed in sweat, I was carried down from the platform, a magical bishop.

Hugo Ball, *Flight Out of Time*

Ball's most intense performance was also one of his last. With Hennings, he officially quit the Dadas (although he became reconciled with Tzara in the year 1917). The two retired to a small Swiss village near Ascona to write and study mystical Catholic texts.

Ball and Hennings were soon replaced by other young German artists. Dada evidently had a life of its own and a widening reputation. At their new Galerie Dada in Zurich, the Dadas found financial support for their artworks and publications—reportedly a band of old Swiss women were behind them. Their performance series continued—there were five more soirees in 1917—but the Dada sense of the unexpected became framed in a more literary and artistic fashion as they added marionettes, Rudolf von Laban's dancers, and even playscripts like Oskar Kokoschka's *Sphinx and Strawman*. Dada's aggressive return to the anarchy of nature and childhood needed more virgin soil to dig. Only their final production on April 9, 1919 provides the shock of madness and violence they needed as a send-off from Zurich. Here, Hans Richter described Walter Serner's closing action on that evening.

> Suddenly, Serner, carrying a headless dummy, made his entrance. Placing the dummy down, he went back behind the curtain and returned bearing a bunch of artifical flowers which he motioned for the dummy to smell. Laying the flowers at the dummy's feet, he then proceeded to sit in a chair in the middle of the stage with his back to the audience and to recite from the nihilistic tract "Final Dissolution."

> The tension in the hall became unbearable. At first it was so quiet that you could hear a pin drop. Then the catcalls began, scornful at first, then furious. "Rat, bastard, you've got a nerve!" until the noise almost entirely drowned Serner's voice, which could be heard, during a momentary lull, saying the words, "Napoleon was a big strong oaf, after all."

> That really did it. What Napoleon had to do with it, I don't know. He wasn't Swiss. But the young men, most of whom were in the gallery, leaped on the stage, brandishing pieces of the balustrade (which had survived intact for several hundred years), chased Serner into the wings and out of the building, smashed the tailor's dummy and the chair, and stamped on the bouquet. The whole place was in an uproar.

> Hans Richter, *Dada: Art and Anti-Art*

Dada in Berlin, 1918-1920

Just as the Galerie Dada started up in January 1917, a depressed Richard Huelsenbeck returned to his native Berlin. Huelsenbeck's exact reasons are unclear. True, his father was sick and he wanted to begin his medical studies. Still, it seems that the Cabaret Voltaire was something of a pre-graduate school fling for Huelsenbeck. During the entire year of 1917, however, Dada, with Tzara at the helm, began to receive newspaper notoriety in a battle-weary Central Europe.

In early 1918, Huelsenbeck saw an opportunity to trade on his experiences at the Cabaret Voltaire. He organized an art and poetry evening at the Graphisches Kabinett for February 18. Lecturing on Dada's meaning and history before a curious, but slightly fearful audience, Huelsenbeck started to recite some of his *Lautgedichte* as literary samples. That did it. The gallery's spectators began to stir. The proprietor, J. B. Neumann was already at the telephone, threatening to call the police. Huelsenbeck's friends immediately intervened. As a rebuff to Neumann, Huelsenbeck shouted out that the Dadas were in favor of war and the last one was not bloody enough. Suddenly, a veteran with a wooden leg stood up and left. The audience responded with applause, which caused Huelsenbeck to shout even more vociferously, inexplicably attacking the Cubists and Futurists. Again the audience was confused—the Dada revolution was spreading to new lands.

Other poets continued the evening, uncertain as to the audience's mood and the proper response. The painter of the grotesque, George Grosz, recited his works—really rhymed insults—then clutched his groin and began to violently pace before some Expressionist paintings. To the disbelief of the audience, Grosz pretended to relieve himself on one of the portraits. More astonishing still was Grosz's shouted contention that what he was doing was artistically correct since urine was a superior varnish. Huelsenbeck returned to read more poetry. The restless spectators stood—either in protest or confusion—and Huelsenbeck lashed out at them, "What are you waiting for? The next downfall of Germany? Aren't you satisfied with enough victims? Sit down!" Many of the Berlin's newspapers carried the Dada story on their front pages during the next two days. One editor asked outright, what on earth is Dada?

On April 12, 1918, the Dada-scandal was repeated. Joined by Raoul Hausmann and several other young artists, Huelsenbeck led off with a frenzied attack on Expressionism. He redefined Dada in the most provocative terms but the spectators remained calm. Grosz recited his insults. Still nothing. Finally, Else Hadwinger started to read a Marinetti poem extolling the virtues of war, to which Huelsenbeck provided a musical accompaniment on a toy trumpet and rattle. A soldier in a field-gray uniform fell to the floor in an epileptic seizure. Hausmann got up to read his lecture, "The New Materials in Painting" but the incongruity must have been too great; someone switched the lights off, creating a panic and an end to the evening.

Although the Berlin Dadas divided along political lines—roughly between anarchist and Communist (Spartakist Party) tendencies—during the year-long crisis between April 1918 and April 1919, their costumed presence was felt everywhere as they shouted their slogans and peddled their magazines. In the oddest places in Berlin, one could find their stickers, "Dada kicks you in the ass and you like it!" or "What have the *gentlemen* done with the stage?" On April 1, two weeks after the slaughter of 1500 German revolutionaries, the Dadas jokingly declared a "Dada-Republik of Berlin-Nikolassee." An entire regiment of Noske's civil troops were held in readiness for them.

With the settling of the political scene, several massive Dada revue performances were mounted during April and May 1919. Mostly they were a series of crazy contests, *Lautgedichte*, atonal music, and the usual poetic provocations. (Ben Hecht's description of the May 15 Dada-Soiree appears in the document section.) Sometimes Grosz would walk through the audience haranguing them, and then demand money for his artistry. Usually the performances ended in violence with spectators tossing objects at the performers and charging the stage. Every newspaper had its own theory about Dada and its new satiric art of photo-montage. There were even pseudo-Dada societies created by intellectuals who were refused membership in the real Berlin Dada group.

The Dadas attracted Max Reinhardt's interest when they demonstrated outside his newly-built Grosse Schauspielhaus. Reinhardt astutely invited Walter Mehring to write for his cabaret, *Schall und Rauch*. Mehring's witty Dada chansons led to other programs there, and in December 1919, the Dadas presented a complete evening of "dancing, recitations, sketches, cartoons, and a political puppet show." The Dadas' growing entertainment professionalism got the better of them as the audience respectfully applauded each act. Mehring's puppet performance of *Simply Classical! An Orestia With a Happy Ending* attempted to parody Reinhardt's spectacle *Orestia*, then playing at the Grosse Schauspielhaus. (One critic wrote, "Aeschylus above, Aristophanes below.") Mehring's marionettes were designed by Grosz as current political figures and types of the Weimar Republic and international scene. Historically, it was the first—or one of the first—theatrical productions to integrate motion picture footage with live action. So pleasant was the production that the Dadas themselves had to attack their own evening, shouting, "Down with Reinhardtism!"

The last major Berlin Dada performance activity was given by Huelsenbeck, Hausmann, and Johannes Baader, a certified lunatic who

already stormed the first Weimar Assembly, declaring himself the Oberdada and President of the Globe. In February and March of 1920, the trio
toured Southern Germany and Czechoslovakia. Huelsenbeck described it in
his 1957 memoir.

> To sum up our reading circuit in a single sentence: we annoyed and
> bewildered our audiences. The one thing in common to all of our
> performances was that we never knew in advance what we were go-
> ing to say. I usually read the *Phantastische Gebete* and Hausmann,
> as far as I can remember always had his sound poems on hand. But
> this material naturally couldn't fill out an evening. So from the
> very start, we had to make the audience realize that it shouldn't ex-
> pect very much . . . Before the performance, I would step over to
> the edge of the podium and call out: "Ladies and Gentlemen . . . if
> you think that we have come here to sing or recite something, then
> you are the victims of an unfortunate error." . . . People called out
> that they wanted to see Dada. "Dada is nothing," I said. "We
> ourselves don't know what Dada is . . ." Someone would call out
> "get the police." "Ladies and Gentlemen," I said, "not even the
> police can change the fact that we do not intend to offer you enter-
> tainment such as you generally get in the movies or in the theatre."
> —Richard Huelsenbeck, *Memoirs of a Dada Drummer*

Dada in Cologne and Hanover, 1918-1923

The political and cultural upheavals that made Dada a serious newspaper
topic in 1919 were unique to Berlin, but Dada spread elsewhere in Weimar
Germany—albeit in more artistic and literary forms. In British-occupied
Cologne during the years 1919 and 1920, Max Ernst, Johannes Baargeld,
and Arp with a half-dozen local artists terrorized the local censors and
cultural authorities. The founder of the Rhineland Communist party and its
journal, *Der Ventilator*, the young Baargeld became persuaded by Ernst
that Dada was far more revolutionary. Baargeld's wealthy father, anxious
to wean his son away from the embarrassing and dangerous political scene,
funded their early Dada ventures, which centered around journal-making
and exhibitions of their photo-montages and collage-littered canvases. For
the most part, the Cologne Dadas shocked the local bourgeoisie with
bizarre and disquieting graphic works. When they weren't signing each
other's paintings, Baargeld produced impossible line-and-newspaper-paste-
up montages. Ernst invented a grainy rub-on technique that he soon applied
to the distorted nineteenth-century block images of horror and flight, in the
manner of de Chirico.

In March 1919, the Cologne Dadas created their first public scandal, by interrupting a recitation of Expressionist poetry, given at the municipal theatre. The Dada's only recorded performance activity occurred at their second official exhibition in April 1920. Ernst and Baargeld rented a glassed-in court on the opposite end of a beer-hall pissoir. There, a girl, dressed as if for her first communion, recited an obscene poem. Around her were various art objects, such as a skull, an alarm clock, and a hand emerging from a pool of red liquid. Another assemblage made of wood had a hatchet attached to it, inviting any critic to destroy it. The commotion created by the unsuspecting urinal-users attracted the attention of the Cologne police, who assumed they were breaking up a homosexual gathering. The Dada-exhibition was closed for one day when the only objectionable object turned out to be a miniature of Dürer's *Adam and Eve*.

In June 1918, Kurt Schwitters (1887-1948) left his native Hanover for Berlin, where he hoped to join with Rudolf Blümner and others of the Expressionist Sturm-school. But as Berlin Expressionism seemed to move away from abstraction, Schwitters began to correspond with Arp and Tzara in Zurich. They suggested that he meet with Huelsenbeck and others of the Club Dada in Berlin. Instinctively, Grosz took an immediate and life-long dislike for the apolitical Schwitters. Officially, he was never to be admitted into the society of Dada.

In Schwitters, the paradox of Dada became apparent. Although the Dadas saw themselves as the shock troops and guardians of an anti-art, anti-bourgeois revolution, their eccentric behavior, poetry, paintings, typography, and performances had quickly developed into a discernible style. There was even a growing audience for it. Despite his Sturm background, Schwitters's work closely resembled that of the Dadas' in Zurich, Berlin, and Cologne. Only his public behavior differed: Schwitters thought of himself as an artist. In July 1919, Schwitters announced his own Dada-like movement, MERZ. The word was playfully taken from an advertisement for COMMERZBANK that appeared in one of his complex and beautifully designed assemblages, made of the flotsam and litter of popular culture and found objects.

Like Ball, Schwitters rejected the delimited world of dramatic and literary theatre for an abstract *Gesamtkunstwerk*. In a certain way, his MERZ collages and assemblages were just miniature versions of his MERZ-Stage, which called for the dense inter-mixing of sounds, mechanical devices, transforming and combustible materials, people, flickering light and color sources, human articles of clothing, and occasional texts. Schwitters's MERZ-Stage was never created but several versions of his Dada-like manifesto for it appeared in four publications in 1919. What Schwitters did create were MERZ performances of poetry and his MERZ-Bau, a growing architectonic construction that slowly devoured his two-storied house in Hanover. (Each room was given a special name, such as the Cathedral of

Erotic Misery, and contained hollowed-out columns with assemblage effects of photographs, eyeglasses, hair, letters, etc., of various individuals.)

By and large, Schwitters's MERZ performances followed the styles and formats already set by the Berlin Dadas. When he traveled with Hausmann to southern Germany and Czechoslovakia in the fall of 1921, their MERZ/ANTI-DADA evenings consisted of Dada-like recitations with a few practical jokes. Curiously, the audiences were nicely behaved and seemed to enjoy themselves. For one, Schwitters's well-modulated voice and sense of showmanship revealed a kind of pleasant artistry that would have irritated Huelsenbeck and his Berlin provocateurs. On his Dutch tour in January 1923, Schwitters responded to the question of "What is Dada?" by barking one night and blowing his nose on the next night. At the first performance, pandemonium broke out as applause gave way to jeering and fainting. The next day, one Dutch paper defined Dada as "bark." Schwitters's charm and ingenuity—one poem demonstration consisted only of Schwitters's sound improvisations on the letter "W"—brought an artistry and sophistication to MERZ that rarely was associated with the Dada of Germany.

Dada in Paris, 1920-24

In Paris, Dada reached its literary apogee and final destination. It began characteristically with a periodical. In 1919, Louis Aragon, André Breton, and Philippe Soupault founded the modernist journal, *Littérature*. They were excited about Tzara's Dada activities in Zurich and invited him to publish a Dada poem in *Littérature*. Francis Picabia, the Spanish painter, who had met Tzara in Zurich, testified to his magnetic personality and, with others of the *Littérature* group, implored him to come to Paris. On January 17, 1920, Tzara arrived.

Although Breton and his group understood Dada's intellectual absolutism, its artistic anarchy and power of provocation, they found themselves somewhat shy and fearful of Tzara's unbridled showmanship and abilities to create scandal. Advertising its first program as a matinee of lectures, poetry, modern music, and contemporary art, the first Paris Dada performance was given on January 23. Reading and reciting their works amidst the abandoned set pieces of an amateur theatre production, the avant-garde French poets and writers pretty much gave the audience what they had expected. Then Aragon announced a surprise: the unlisted Tzara would recite a manifesto. Suddenly, Tzara appeared and began reading a political speech from the morning paper as Breton and Aragon rang bells that covered Tzara's Rumanian accent. The art-loving spectators went berserk, whistling and shouting at Tzara's lying effrontery. Even some of the experimental poets found themselves shocked at Tzara's outrageous anti-art gesture. The Dada revolution had secured a stronghold in Paris.

The second and third Dada Matinees on February 5 and 7 played themselves out according to the public expectations. At the February 5 program, which promised the presence of Charlie Chaplin, a half-dozen Dada manifestos were read as spectators shouted, threw coins to the stage, set off flashing powder, and one pregnant woman fainted. The lights had to be brought down on Tzara to fend off a genuine riot. The February 7 performance began with a riot before the Dadas got in an offensive word. At a French workers club, two weeks later, the Dadas harangued against modern poetry and Cubism. Only their attack on Marx and Lenin brought the workers to their feet. But, for the first time, the Paris Dadas failed to elicit a strong audience response.

The great Dada evening on March 27 revealed the Paris Dada's affinity for theatrical sketches and plays. Celebrating the twenty-fifth anniversary of Jarry's *Ubu Roi* at the Théâtre de l'Oeuvre, the Dadas now attracted a sold-out audience of over 1200. The first part of the evening consisted of very short dramatic and musical pieces. In one Dada sketch, a ventriloquist performed three separate characters. The writer and former painter, Georges Ribemont-Dessaignes composed a chance piano score by recording the melody and harmony notations from the random spins of a pin or roulette wheel. Entitled "No Endive," Ribemont-Dessaignes's unmelodious and disharmonious composition was played by the cousin of Picabia's wife as spectators shouted and blew high-pitched whistles. In darkness, Breton read Picabia's manifesto, which in part defined Dada:

> Dada, it doesn't smell. It means nothing,
> Absolutely nothing. Dada is like your hopes: Nothing!
> Like your paradise: Nothing!
> Like your idols: Nothing!
> Like your politicians: Nothing!
> Like your leaders: Nothing!
> Like your artists: Nothing!
> Like your religion: Nothing!
> Hiss, shout, kick my teeth in. So what?
> I shall still tell you fools that in three months, my friends
> and I will be selling you our picture for Francs.

In the second part of the Dada-Soiree, Ribemont-Dessaignes's *The Mute Canary* was staged as Breton, playing the part of Riquet, perched himself on the top rung of a ladder, the production's only set piece. Soupault as Ocre appeared in blackface. By now the audience's frenzy made Ribemont-Dessaignes's wordplay all but unintelligible. The evening's final and third part consisted of a manifesto by Ribemont-Dessaignes, the second act of Breton and Soupault's *If You Please*, and a new performance of Tzara's *The First Celestial Adventure of Mr. Antipyrine*, in which the performers recited inside huge sack-like costumes. Twisted ropes and a bicycle wheel comprised the play's entire scenic design. The soiree ended with a showing of Picabia's "Portrait of Cezanne" (a stuffed monkey) and a soprano's serious pleas to sing Duprac's *Clair de lune*. All in all, the Dada-Soiree was a complete success. (In the excitement that followed, Lugné-Poe announced his readiness to produce Dada playscripts.)

The largest Dada demonstration in Paris, the Dada Festival, took place at the prestigious Salle Gaueau on May 26, 1920. Its publicity campaign, which included Breton walking the streets as a "sandwich-man," was the most aggressive yet. "Sodomistic" music was to be played; all Dadas were to cut off their hair in public; the "sex" of Dada was to be revealed. (This turned out to be a large cardboard cylinder affixed to two shrinking balloons.) Other balloons and cylinders carried the names of the enemies and founders of Paris Dada. Ribemont-Dessaignes wore an inverted funnel on his head that caught the vegetables, eggs, and beefsteaks thrown by the spectators. Two plays were presented that evening, Tzara's *The Second Celestial Adventure of Mr. Antipyrine* and Breton and Soupault's *You Would Have Forgotten*. Eggs were tossed once again as Tzara concluded the Festival with his "Vaseline Symphony," an extended *Lautgedichte* with ten performers entoning "Cra . . . cra" and "Cri . . . cri."

The simple question of how the Paris Dadas were to follow up on the outrageous Dada Festival success turned into a crisis that would split the movement. Tzara's insistence on the repetition of the formats of the March and May soirees—with *Fourth and Fifth Adventures of Antipyrine*—made little sense to the French Dadas. Their sense of the unexpected and creative spontaneity was dissipating. At first, Picabia resigned, issuing a communique in the papers; then others slowly lost interest. In 1920 and 1921, the Paris Dadas performed in non-theatrical environments: in churches, the morgue, a train station; they staged a mock trial of progressive-turned-bourgeois writer, Maurice Barres. On June 6, 1921, they staged another evening of performance provocations, which included the mounting of Tzara's *The Gas Heart*, where characters enacted a part of the body.

By the fall of 1922, Breton himself had officially broken from Tzara and Dada. For Breton and his comrades, Dada's negativity was no longer a creative force; a year-and-a-half later, Surrealism would replace it. It was at this time that Roger Vitrac wrote *Free Entry*, a play that moved in the vacuum of Dada and Surrealism, displaying elements of both movements. Dada was declared dead, but Tzara continued.

On July 6, 1923, *The Gas Heart* was restaged at the Théâtre Michel in a professional-looking production that featured costumes by Sonia

Delaunay. Breton and other ex-Dadas jumped on the stage injuring performers and smashing set pieces. In the house, Breton's supporters fought Tzara's defenders. Breton himself was arrested for breaking the arm of a new Dada poet. Tzara's last Dada production, *Handkerchief of Clouds*, however, failed to create any such response and even demonstrated to the supreme egotist himself his total isolation from the French avant-garde. Presented at the Théâtre de la Cigale on May 17, 1924, Tzara's play did achieve a certain literary and comic value but possibly for that very reason produced little excitement. Its chief innovation consisted of keeping the stage hands and offstage actors in full view of the audience.

The final Dada-like activity in Paris (and in Europe) took place on December 4, 1924. This was Picabia's notorious *Relâche*. Although for most Parisian spectators Dada's moment had long past, *Rêlache* brought together Dada's acid humor and ability to reassemble the conventions of art and theatre on novel and electrifying means. Staged by Rolf de Maré of the Swedish Ballet, *Relâche* created confusion and outrage at every level. French for "No Performance" (or "relax"), the title *Relâche* caused many of the Swedish Ballet's patrons to jump back into their limousines on opening night, assuming the performance was cancelled. The production they missed captured all the clever absurdity and willful madness of the entire Dada movement. *Relâche* began with a film prologue by a young René Clair and music by Erik Satie. After one minute, hundreds of lights in photographic metallic reflectors blinded the audience. These formed the backdrop. On the stage, dozens of disconnected activities were enacted. A fireman for the theatre smoked cigarettes and poured water from one pail to another. Man Ray, the American artist, sat on the side of the stage, occasionally marking off space with his shoes. Figures from Cranach's "Adam and Eve" appeared. Tuxedoed playboys disrobed. And an automobile brought on a young couple in evening clothes. During the twenty-minute intermission, Clair's Dada film was projected on a lowered screen. The final curtain displayed the flashing names and graphics of *Relâche*'s producers and artists. It proved to be both the end of the Swedish Ballet and Dada.

1916 - 1924

Dada's Pre-History

Posters advertising
attractions for
Impressions of Africa

Raymond Roussel's
Impressions of Africa, 1912

No play text of *Impressions of Africa* survives today. The performance differed considerably from Roussel's 1910 novel of the same name, with more characters and an inverted sequence of events. Abba Cherniack-Tzuriel's synopsis was constructed from several sources other than the novel; these include newspaper reviews, Roussel's later comments, and an extant cue sheet of the character, Juillard, published in a special Roussel issue of *Bizarre* no. 34-35, 1964 (Paris).

Impressions of Africa:
A Description

Prologue—A Beach

The curtain rises. Through a stormy night, shadows are seen moving about on an African beach. There are flashes of lightning that reveal a backdrop showing a ship in distress. Thunder is heard. A voice calls out, "When will the boat be full? Take the passengers to the beach." The curtain falls. The prologue has lasted about five minutes.

Act One: *A Site in Equatorial Africa*

Baia, the black fool, speaking in gibberish language, conducts several men and two women onto the stage that is now a site in Equatorial Africa. In the backdrop can be seen the wreck of a ship in the center and tropical trees at its sides. The men are wearing white clothes or khaki dolmans as is the custom in the tropics. The women wear the fashionable dresses and hats of the style of the turn-of-the-century. They stand to the right of the stage.

Juillard, the natural leader of the shipwrecked Europeans and an historian, played by Duard, a well-known actor, ignoring Baia, says, "Finally! Saved! But prisoners, and of whom?" Juillard then assures one of the Europeans that their fate, "won't take long to work itself out." Formally assuming leadership, he asks Carmichael if there are any wounded, and upon hearing that only one person is wounded in the shoulder, inquires about his favorite, Dodor. He is told that Dodor, a young Parisian electrician and the white counterpart to Baia, is well. Apparently one of the people present speaks of putting up resistance against their African captors, but Juillard agrees with Dodor, who has just entered the stage, " . . . Mr. Dodor, a sound piece of advice, let's not create hatreds, we are at their mercy."

Juillard addresses Baia, saying that as he speaks a little French he might tell them who his master is and where they are. Baia tells them they must pay a ransom before they are released, but it will take many weeks before they can get the money from Europe.

There is a change of scene as Talou VII, majestically dressed in purple, approaches in a solemn manner at the head of a phalanx of black warriors and women. The actors stand in a semi-circle and speak across to each other. Talou wears a sort of Indian feather headdress attached to a European-style crown. He tries to appear pleasant at all times, and he pronounces the "e" at the end of his words, implying a misunderstanding of French grammar and pronunciation, which one critic interpreted as an English accent. Juillard compliments him on his knowledge of French.

Talou then invites the Europeans to introduce themselves. Juillard begins by explaining his unique position as an historian,

> I profit from a situation of independent fortune to undertake continual travels and in this way to prepare some lectures, some work. (*Smiling.*) I will be happy about the circumstances that unite us in order to add to my last work this unforeseen page.

Juillard continues his speech, describing the shipwreck itself; how their boat, the *Lyncee*, carrying a large group of performers, musicians, inventors, scientists, and freaks, who were on their way to Buenos Aires, was wrecked by a hurricane. Unlike Talou, Juillard speaks very rapidly while calmly smiling. He is evidently barely understood by some spectators.

The others introduce themselves. These include Carmichael, a male soprano who performs in cabarets in drag; Bex, a chemist and an inventor of strange machines; Adinolfa, a tragic actress with "incomparably clear" diction (actually played by a comedienne); Skarioffszky, who has a special kind of zither; Olga Chernonenkova, a fat Latvian ballet dancer with a moustache, who previously rode on her pet elk; Soureau, an actor; Jenn, the ringmaster; Bedu, another inventor; and Chenevillot, an architect.

Talou now tells the complicated history of dissension and civil strife growing out of the struggle between two sons born at the same moment to Spanish twin sisters marooned on the coast many generations before. He weeps when he speaks of his beloved daughter, Sirdah, who is blind. Juillard makes a few comments about the story Talou has told and says he knows by reputation the famous explorer, Felicien Laube, whom Talou had mentioned. When Talou and his entourage leave, Juillard tells of his plans to set up a club called "The Incomparables":

> My friends, during these two months we will have to fight against a terrible enemy, boredom—that, in these regions, is, for white men, a true plague that can lead to the worst catastrophe, to sickness, to bloody quarrels, it is necessary to amuse ourselves, no matter what and continuously. For this reason I propose to start an unusual club, in which each member will have to distinguish himself by an original work.

He accepts the post of president of the club and tells the shipwrecked Europeans that they will put on a gala performance when they are finally liberated. Juillard proposes that Chenevillot, an architect, build a theatre for them

> that will be in some way an emblem of the group and that, in view of the future exhibitions, will have the form of a slightly raised stage.

The curtain lowers on the first act.

Act Two

After the Europeans are assigned to their quarters, Dodor surprises a young black couple who are hiding there. This is Djizmé, favorite of the minister Mossem, and Nair, who always wears a bowler hat. An envious person gives them away by stealing Nair's hat and writing the word "pincee" (a pinch of something) in white on it. As this person ran under Djizmé's window, she touched the hat and the letter "p" was left on her gray glove, which she never took off. Her husband was warned and, though at first he doesn't pay attention, as he loves the empress, Rul, he finally traps the couple, and Djizme is condemned to die an adulteress' death.

In the next scene, still early in the morning, Juillard descends with Bex, the scientist, looking for "that good Dodor." Juillard, in reply to something Bex has said about the passing native women, replies, "Yes, indeed, they have a charming way of carrying the jugs on their heads or on their hips."

He then sees Baia and Dodor arguing in another part of the stage. Baia and Dodor are constantly at loggerheads in these first two acts. Juillard tells Bex that Chenevillot has finished the theatre, which is like a standard Punch and Judy stage. Juillard says that Michael has already tested the acoustics dressed in "his feminine fashion." When Juillard is asked what kind of medal he has made up, he replies that he has chosen to make an original and simple sign. He suggests that there be six small medals made in the triangular shape of the Greek letter, delta. Juillard explains to Bex, Carmichael, and Dodor that "without changing the model, I've cut in the same zinc plate, a giant beta, made to be worn around the neck . . . designed for the most worthy."

The second scene ends with Juillard letting Dodor know that he had missed one "of Talou's recitations" the evening before. Juillard tells Bex not to tease "this good man Dodor." Suddenly, they are all greeted by the approaching European women.

The men rise to greet the ladies who are carrying flowers and Juillard remarks that they are early risers. Someone mentions the story of the disappearance of Sirdau, Talou's blind daughter. A long discussion now takes place between Juillard, Bex, Carmichael, Adinolfa, Olga, and Louise about how Talou has been betrayed by his empress, Rul, the mother of Sirdah. The gossip (or exposition) includes the telling of how Sirdah was kidnapped and abandoned in the jungle by Rul and her lover, Mossem, Talou's chief minister. The Europeans narrate the exotic story of how Rul, jealous of her daughter's comeliness, caused her to be blind again. Gathering some magic plants from a place used by a witch doctor, Rul rubbed them on the eyelashes of Sirdah. However, Rul was caught in the act by the palace guards and then imprisoned. The next day Talou took Sirdah to the witch doctor Bachkon to obtain a cure, but the sorcerer refused to help him. Yaour IX, the distant cousin of Talou, wanted Sirdah to marry him and withheld the cure that was found on his side of the river. Talou refuses to consent to this marriage and returns with Sirdah to Ejur.

In the next scene Juillard sees Sirdah and greets her, but she wants to go off by herself. It may be at this time that Sirdah has a long "touching" conversation with Dodor. Juillard, in the next scene, hears that Yaour's envoy, who has been sent to talk to Talou has betrayed Yaour's plans, which were to invade Ponukele and kill Talou. Juillard sees that trouble is brewing and asks some of the Europeans if they have firearms. Someone replies that he still has a revolver. The Europeans decide to stick together in the face of the coming struggle. In scene six, Juillard tells Sirdah to stay with the Europeans and not to think of running away. Somewhat frantically, Sirdah reveals to Juillard that she had dreamt of public executions and prefers to remain blind rather than witness such a day. Sirdah's monologue, according to a critic, was highly effective.

In the presence of Sirdah, Juillard, and the others, Talou enters dressed in the gown of the tragedienne Adinolfa and in a blonde wig. Yaour has appeared and, seeing Talou thus arrayed, demands to have a woman's costume as well. He is given the costume of Marguerite from *Faust*, which includes a blonde wig with one long braid, but before they commence the combat, each removes the costume. After a few moments of fierce fighting, Talou defeats Yaour. Juillard congratulates Talou on his victory, and there is talk of a marriage, though it is not clear whose, as the curtain comes down on the second act.

Act Three. *The Behuliphruen* (a special area in the jungle)

There are black actors, Europeans in black face, and Europeans on stage before a backdrop showing an exotic Rousseau-like jungle area. It is during this time that the eight "acts" are performed as part of the contest held by "The Incomparables Club" for which the medals in the shape of a delta and a beta will be awarded.

Eight of the twelve "attractions" shown on the poster are performed in Act Three. [Depicted at the beginning of this section.]

1. *The Earthworm Zither Player*

This attraction was probably the best known of the twelve, appearing in a light-hearted cartoon that attempted to summarize the essential points of the play in *Le Rire* on May 25, 1912. The zither scene was also shown in an early photograph published in *Le Figaro* in September 1911.

The zither was worked by having a giant earthworm crawl across the top of the inside of a glass case, thereby releasing drops or streams of heavy, mercury-like water that struck the cords of the instrument. The man standing in both the sketch and the photograph with a conductor's stick was Skarioffszky, who was dressed in a tight-fitting, red Tzigane outfit. He created the machine and apparently trained the earthworm to perform.

2. The Dwarf Philippo Whose Normally-Developed Head Equals in Height the Rest of His Body.

In the inset of the upper right corner in the sketch, Philippo's head is seen on a kind of double platter without a body. Presumably the body is concealed between the two disks. Philippo speaks and sprays a great deal of saliva on all those observing him as his head—and body—are handed around to the actor-spectators. The hand shown in the sketch belongs to Jenn, the ringmaster, who introduces Philippo.

3. The One-Legged Lelgoualch Playing the Flute Made of His Own Tibia.

The one-legged Breton, Lelgoualch, appears in traditional folk costume. Previously, Lelgoualch had climbed to the top of a greasy pole during a festival and fell; he did not tell anyone that he had broken his leg and eventually lost it. The flute he plays was made from the tibia of his amputated leg. In the cartoon from *Le Rire*, he is shown riding along in a small wagon.

4. The Wall of Dominos Evoking Priests.

By using dominos, coins and cards, Whirligig, a light and slender clown with flour on his face, constructs three images portraying "a group of reverend gentlemen leaving the tower of an old cloister to visit the parish priest in his rectory." Presumably the priest's image was created painstakingly by piecing together the many pieces of domino to build a kind of unsupported wall. The uniform rectangles arranged one deep, were placed on top of each other in perfect symmetry, many with their black sides showing, the rest turned outwards, their white faces showing various numbers of spots.

5. The Thermo-mechanic Orchestra Made of Bexium.

Using a "new metal, chemically endowed . . . with a prodigious thermal sensitivity," the inventor Bex constructs a complicated music machine that works through the application of heat and cold. It is possible, in fact, that the instrument produced sounds "by virtue of an electric motor concealed in its interior," as suggested by Roussel.

6. The Wind Clock of Never-Never-Land

The wind-clock was run by constant and predictable daily wind currents. Its appearance was that of a clock-face cut by a third. At each horizontal end of the dial are the words "Noon," in the center of the bottom rim "Midnight." Accordingly, the breeze would bow the solitary hand across the dial, indicating the time, the east wind changing to west each noon and midnight.

7. The Cats Playing the Game of "Prisoners"

Trained by Marius Bucharessas, a ten-year-old boy, in the manner of a standard vaudevillian act, a collection of small cats performed a series of complicated actions. Wearing green and red ribbons, the cats formed two teams according to their respective colors. At a sign from Bucharessas, the two groups proceeded to play a game of Prisoner's Base, as the boy established boundaries with his foot.

8. The Echoing Chests of the Alcott Brothers

The father of the six Alcott Brothers, Stephen, calls out four syllables: "Ste . . . phen Al . . . cott." This is repeated six times at six points of an enormous zig-zag without the participants making the slightest movement with their lips. It is the voice of the head of the family that reverberates against the thoracic cavities of the six brothers. Reportedly, this is made possible due to their extreme emaciation, carefully maintained by a rigorous diet, allowing the bone-hard surfaces of the brothers' chests to reflect all sound vibrations.

After a good deal of jeering and coin throwing from the real audience, the grand prize of the "giant beta" is awarded to the ten-year-old Marius Bucharessas and his performing cats, the "act" that brought about the most enthusiastic response from the Ponukelian spectators.

Act Four. *The backdrop shows the Square of the Trophies*

A critic described the decor of act four as including "potted plants on the stage with heads hung in the branches like Christmas lights." Four of the twelve "attractions" advertised in the poster are presented in act four, and other "attractions" are also performed.

Norbert and Louise Montalescot, a brother and sister who had previously fallen into the hands of Talou after being abandoned by their guides in the jungle, successfully demonstrate:

The Statue of Whale Bones from a Corset on Rails Made from a Calf's Lung.

This is the "dummy . . . that moved . . . a little bit" that Duchamp remembered. It is a statue made by the minor character Norbert Montalescot with the help of his sister Louise, a chemist. If he does not succeed in making it move in a certain way, Talou will neither release him nor his sister. Norbert is instructed by Talou to make a statue so light that it could be moved by the slightest touch of Louise's pet magpie. The contraption is made of whale bones taken from ladies corsets found in the shipwreck. It must be light enough to glide back and forth over tracks made of inflated calf's lungs. The statue itself represents the "Death of Saridakis" where the helot Saridakis is struck with a dagger by his frustrated teacher since Saridakis is unable to conjugate a simple auxiliary verb. Just as Saridakis's heart is pierced, he becomes a statue.

Louise is dressed in military uniform. She wears an

> officer's pelisse, the gold shoulder knots of which dissimulate the hollow surgical needles that penetrate her right lung and give rise to a peculiar kind of automatic music upon each effort she makes to breathe.

This was an acting situation that the critic of *Comoedia illustré*, on June 1, 1912, acknowledged as "sufficiently dangerous." Satisfied with the workings of their machine, Talou releases them. The reviewer for *Journal des Debats* wrote:

> As to the sculptor condemned to raise a statue that wouldn't break a veal lung, he succeeded in assembling a carcass of blubber. One regrets that he didn't have the idea of inflating this statue . . . anyway he is saved.

Seil-Kor, a young black who, having fallen in love with the daughter of the famous explorer, Felicien Laubé, has been quite mad since her death some time before. The white doctor stretches him out under a vine arbor garnished with a certain hypno-genetic plant and shows Seil-Kor, "in a vision," the portrait of the one that he loved. Slides or projections reveal the subconscious thoughts or events that happened in the past. Seeing the slide-vision of his dead beloved immediately returns Seil-Kor's sanity to him.

Carmichael, the male soprano in drag, who has been forced to memorize an epic hymn, written by Talou, called "Jeroukka," sings it.

After this, the public tortures and punishments begin to be meted out.

Djizmé Voluntarily Electrocuted by Lightning

The electric bed-table or bed lightning-conductor—the kind of contraption "you might see at a traveling fair"—was invented by the humane scientist, Bex, as an improbable punishment for the adultress, Djizmé. Counting on the rarity of storms in that part of Africa, thereby preventing an execution, Box places a lightning rod at the head of a "copper cradle." Unfortunately, as Djizmé "nonchalantly stretches out" on the special bed-table, placing her head in the iron cap and her feet in metal shoes, a storm approaches.

The Punishment of the Pins

Talou's faithless empress, Rul, is tortured to death. The golden pins from her hair are pressed into her body through the eyelets of a red knotted and frayed corset she wears. This corset and the pins have been taken off the body of a Swiss woman whom she and Talou had seen floating in the ocean after a shipwreck.

The Body of the Black King Yaour IX at the Foot of a Decaying Tree, Costumed Classically as Marguerite in Faust

Finally there is the triumphant celebration of Talou VII's victory over Yaour IX. Talou places his foot on the embalmed cross-dressed body of Yaour: this supreme humiliation causes Talou's women to frantically undulate. The victory dance is accompanied throughout by belches, since the women had just finished eating a communal meal from one pot of food.

Sirdah then receives permission to dance in honor of the event, a dance performance that one reviewer described as "a rather mediocre little dance." Talou gives the Europeans their liberty, and the curtain is lowered on the last act.

CABARET
VOLTAIRE
ZURICH
1916-17

Cabaret Voltaire
by Marcel Janco

Cabaret Voltaire Zurich, 1916-17

The Cabaret Voltaire produced few literary texts. Materials from three different evenings in 1916 are collected here to give the reader some varied sense of the Zurich Dadas' earliest activities. These include both play texts and poetry.

The simultaneous poem, "L'amiral cherche une maison à louer" was first performed on March 29, 1916 by Richard Huelsenbeck, Marcel Janco, and Tristan Tzara. The text, which is reprinted here in its original typography, appeared in the journal, Cabaret Voltaire, June 1916. Ball defined this example of the simultaneous poem as "a contrapuntal recitative in which three or more voices speak, sing, whistle, etc., at the same time in such a way that the elegiac, humorous, or bizarre content of the piece is brought out by these combinations."

Ball's A Nativity Play was staged in early June, 1916—probably on June 2—as a Bruitist, or noise, concert. The religious nature of the piece, and what Ball called its "gentle simplicity," caught the cabaret audience, which included Japanese and Turkish tourists, by surprise. Ball found himself embarrassed by the quiet, almost reverential mood that the Nativity Play produced. The text of the piece only includes the first half of eight small sections.

For many of the Dadas, the Authors' Evening of July 14, 1916, held at the Waag Hall, was their most celebrated soiree in Zurich. It brought together nearly all the Dada techniques developed at the Cabaret Voltaire in one representative whole. Included here is a translation of the program (it was not, however, a completely accurate description of the actual evening); two of Emmy Hennings's poems, "Ether" and "Prison"; and two of Ball's Lautgedichte that were recited during that evening. Not listed in the program but performed at the Author's Evening was Tzara's play, The First Celestial Adventure of Mr. Antipyrine, and an accompanying manifesto. (Antipyrine was the trade name of a French headache remedy.) The Tzara play first appeared in Collection Dada, Zurich, 1916.

L'amiral cherche

Poème simultan par R. Huelsenbeck, M. Janko, Tr. Tzara

HUELSENBECK	Ahoi	ahoi	Des	Admirals	gwirktes	Beinkleid	schnell
JANKO, chant			Where	the honny	suckle	wine twines	ilself
TZARA	Boum	boum boum	Il	déshabilla	sa chair	quand les	grenouilles

HUELSENBECK	und	der	Conciergenbäuche	Klapperschlangengrün	sind	milde	ach
JANKO, chant	can	hear	the weopour	will arround	arround	the	hill
TZARA	serpent	à	Bucarest	on dépendra	mes amis	dorénavant	et

HUELSENBECK	prrrza	chrrrza	prrrza		Wer suchet	dem	wird
JANKO, chant	mine	admirabily		confortabily	Grandmother	said	
TZARA					Dimanche:	deux	éléphants

Intermède rythmique

HUELSENBECK	hihi	Yabomm	hihi	Yabomm	hihi	hihi	hihiiiii
	ff		p	cresc ff			cresc ff f
TZARA	rouge	bleu	rouge bleu	rouge bleu	rouge bleu	rouge bleu	
	p			f cresc	ff	cresc	fff
SIFFLET (Janko)	———.	———.		cresc f	—.	ff	—— —.
	p						fff
CLIQUETTE (TZ)	rrrrrrrr	rrrrrrrr	rrrrrrrr	rrrrrrrr	rrrrrrrr	rrrrrrrr	
	f decrsc	f	cresc		fff	uniform	
GROSSE CAISE (Huels.)	O O O	O O O O O	O O O O O	O O O O	O O	
	ff	p	f	fif	p	

HUELSENBECK	im	Kloset	zumeistens	was	er	nötig	hätt	ahoi	iuché	ahoi	iuché
JANKO (chant)	I	love	the	ladies	I	love	to	be	among	the	girls
TZARA	la	concièrge	qui	m'a	trompé	elle a	vendu	l'appartement	que j'avais loué

HUELSENBECK	hätt'	O	süss	gequollnes	Stelldichein	des Admirals	im	Abendschein	uru	uru
JANKO (chant)	o'clock	and	tea	is set I	like	to have	my	tea with	some	brunet	shai	shai
TZARA	Le	train	traîne	la fumée	comme	la fuite	de	l'animal	blessé	aux

HUELSENBECK	Der	Affe	brüllt	die	Seekuh	belt im	Lindenbaum	der Schräg	zerschellt	tara-
JANKO (chant)	doing it	doing	it	see	that	ragtime	coupple	over there	see
TZARA	Autour du	phare	tourne	l'auréole	des oiseaux bleuillis	en moitiés	de lumière	vis-

HUELSENBECK				Peitschen	um	die	Lenden	Im Schlafsack	gröhlt der
JANKO (chant)				oh	yes yes yes	yes yes	yes yes yes		yes	yes
TZARA	cher	c'est	si	difficile	La rue s'enfuit avec mon bagage à traves la ville	Un métro mêle

une maison à louer

zerfällt					Teerpappe	macht	Rawagen			in	der	Nacht
arround	the	door	a	swetheart	mine	is	waiting	patiently	for	me	l
humides	commancèrent	à	bruler	j'ai	mis	le	cheval	dans	l'âme	du

verzerrt   in   der   Natur   chrza   prrrza   chrrrza
                                                                   my   great   room   is
c'est   très   intéressant   les   griffes   des   morsures   équatoriales

aufgetan   Der   Ceylonlöwe   ist   kein   Schwan   Wer   Wasser   braucht   find
                                                        I   love   the   ladies
        Journal   de   Genève   au   restaurant   Le   télégraphiste   assassine

                                                        Find   was   er   nötig
                                                        And   when   it's   five
Dans   l'église   après   la   messe   le   pêcheur   dit   à   la   comtesse :   Adieu   Mathilde

uro   uru   uru   uro   uru   uru   uru   uro   pataclan   patablan   pataplan   uri   uri   uro
shai   shai   shai   shai   shai   shai   Every   body   is doing it   doing it   doing it   Every   body   is
intestins écrasés

tata   tarataia   tatatata   In   Joschiwara   dröhnt   der   Brand   und   knallt   mit   schnellen
that   throw there shoulders in   the   air   She said the raising her heart   oh   dwelling   oh
sant   la distance des batteaux   Tandis   que   les   archanges   chient   et   les   oiseaux   tombent   Oh!   mon

alte   Oberpriester   und   zeigt   der   Schenkel   volle   Tastatur   L'Amiral   n'a   rien   trouvé
yes   oh yes oh yes   oh yes   oh yes   yes yes   oh yes   sir   L'Amiral   n'a   rien   trouvé
   son cinéma la prore de   je   vous adore était au casino du sycomore   L'Amiral   n'a   rien   trouvé

A Nativity Play

Hugo Ball

I. Silent Night

The Wind: f f f f f f f f f fff f ffff t t
Sound of the Silent Night: hummummummummummummummummum
The Shepherds: Hi, hello, hi helloh, hi helloh

Foghorns, Ocarina, Crescendo (*They climb up a mountain*)
the cracking of a whip, cries

The Wind: f f f f f f f f f f f ffffffffffffffffffffffffffffffffffff

II. The Stable

Donkey: ia, ia, ia, ia, ia, ia, ia, ia, ia, ia, ia, ia
Little Ox: muh muh muh muh muh muh muh muh muh muh

(*Stomping, Rustling of Straw, Rattling of Chains, Kicking, Munching*)

Sheep: bah, bah, bah, bah, bah, bah, bah, bah, bah
Joseph and Maria: (*Praying.*) Ramba, ramba, ramba, ramba
    m-barm, m-barm, m-barm, m-barm, bamba, bamba, rambababababa

III. The Apparition of the Angel and the Star

The Star: zoke, zoke, zoke, zzoke, zzzzzoke, zzzzzzzzzzooooooooke,
                    zoke pach, zoke ptsch, zoke ptsch, zoke ptsch
The Angel: (*Sound of a propeller, slowly rising, quivering up to great
    strength, full of energy, demon, demonic*)
Arrival: Hissing, bursting asunder, bundle of light in noises
Light Machine: flushes white white white white white

All who take part are falling / first on the elbow, then on the fists so that
two wings are produced which hang together.

IV. The Annunciation

Sound of Litany: de da de da de da de da de da derum derum derum

(Translated by Henry Marx)

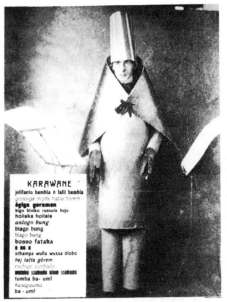

KARAWANE
jolifanto bambla ô falli bambla
grossiga m'pfa habla horem
égiga goramen
higo bloiko russula huju
hollaka hollala
anlogo bung
blago bung
blago bung
bosso fataka
a ss i
schampa wulla wussa ólobo
hej tatta gôrem
eschige zunbada
wulubu ssubudu uluw ssubudu
tumba ba- umf
kusagauma
ba - umf

Hugo Ball performing at the
Cabaret Voltaire, July 14, 1916
Inset of his sound poem,
Karawane

Gadji Beri Bimba

Hugo Ball

gadji beri bimba glandridi laula lonni cadori
gadjama gramma berida bimbala glandri galassassa laulitalomini
gadji beri bin blassa glassala laula lonni cadorsu sassala bim
gadjama tuffm i zimzalla giligla wowolimai bin beri ban
o katalominai rhinozerossola hopsamen laulitalomini hoooo
gadjama rhinozerossola hopsamen
bluku terullala blaulala loooo

zimzim urullala zimzim urullala zimzim zanzibar zimzalla zam
elifantolim brussala bulomen brussala bulomen tromtata
velo da bang bang affalo purzamai affalo purzamai lengado tor
gadjama bimbalo glandridi glassala zingtata pimpalo ögrögööö
viola laxato viola zimbrabim viola uli paluji malooo

tuffm im zimbrabim negramai bumbalo negramai bumbalo tuffm i zim
gadjama bimbala oo beri gadjama gaga di gadjama affalo pinx
gaga di bumbalo bumbalo gadjamen
gaga di bling blong
gaga blung

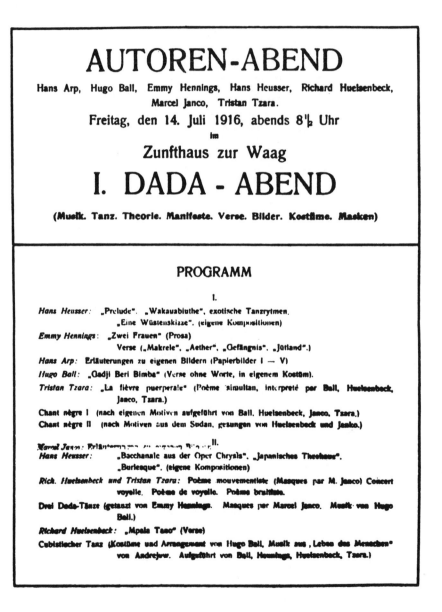

AUTOREN-ABEND

Hans Arp, Hugo Ball, Emmy Hennings, Hans Heusser, Richard Huelsenbeck,
Marcel Janco, Tristan Tzara.

Freitag, den 14. Juli 1916, abends 8½ Uhr

im

Zunfthaus zur Waag

I. DADA - ABEND

(Musik. Tanz. Theorie. Manifeste. Verse. Bilder. Kostüme. Masken)

PROGRAMM

I.

Hans Heusser: „Prelude". „Wakauabluthe", exotische Tanzrytmen.
„Eine Wüstenskizze". (eigene Kompositionen)

Emmy Hennings: „Zwei Frauen" (Prosa)
Verse („Makrele", „Aether", „Gefängnis". „Jütland".)

Hans Arp: Erläuterungen zu eigenen Bildern (Papierbilder I — V)

Hugo Ball: „Gadji Beri Bimba" (Verse ohne Worte, in eigenem Kostüm).

Tristan Tzara: „La fièvre puerperale" (Poème simultan, interpreté par Ball, Huelsenbeck,
Janco, Tzara.)

Chant nègre I (nach eigenen Motiven aufgeführt von Ball, Huelsenbeck, Janco, Tzara.)

Chant nègre II (nach Motiven aus dem Sudan, gesungen von Huelsenbeck und Janko.)

II.

Marcel Janco: Erläuterungen zu eigenen Bildern.

Hans Heusser: „Bacchanale aus der Oper Chrysis". „Japanisches Theehaus".
„Burlesque". (eigene Kompositionen)

Rich. Huelsenbeck und Tristan Tzara: Poème mouvementiste (Masques par M. Janco) Concert
voyelle. Poème de voyelle. Poème bruitiste.

Drei Dada-Tänze (getanzt von Emmy Hennings. Masques par Marcel Janco. Musik von Hugo
Ball.)

Richard Huelsenbeck: „Mpala Tano" (Verse)

Cubistischer Tanz (Kostüme und Arrangement von Hugo Ball, Musik aus „Leben des Menschen"
von Andrejew. Aufgeführt von Ball, Hennings, Huelsenbeck, Tzara.)

Program: July 14, 1916

I.

1.) Hans Heusser: "Prelude," Wakauabluthe" Exotic Dance Rhythms, "A Few Vulgar Sketches" (his compositions)
2.) Emmy Hennings: "Two Women" (prose). "Mackeral," "Ether," "Prison," "Jutland," (poems)
3.) Hans Arp: Lecture on his Pictures (paper pictures 1-4)
4.) Hugo Ball: Dada Manifesto, "Gadji Beri Bimba" (verse without words) in costume
5.) Tristan Tzara: "La fievre puerperale" (simultaneous poem of Ball, Huelsenbeck, Janco, Tzara)
6.) African Chant I (from the motives of Ball, Huelsenbeck, Janco, Tzara)
7.) African Chant II (from motives from the Sudan, sung by Huelsenbeck and Janco)

II.

1.) Marcel Janco: Lecture on his paintings.
2.) Hans Heusser: "Bacchanale from the Opera CHRYSIS," "Japanese Teahouse." "Burlesque" (his composition)
3.) Richard Huelsenbeck and Tristan Tzara: Poem mouvementiste (masks by Janco). Concert voyelle. Poem de voyelle. Poem Bruitiste.
4.) Three Dada Dances (Danced by Hennings. Masks by Janco. Music by Ball).
5.) Richard Huelsenbeck: "Mpala Tano" (poem)
6.) Cubist Dance (Costumes and arrangement by Hugo Ball, music from *The Life of Man* by Andreyev. Performed by Ball, Hennings, Huelsenbeck, Tzara.)

Ether

Emmy Hennings

The rain hits the windows.
A flower lights up red.
Cool air blows against me.
Am I awakening or am I dead?

A world lies far, far away.

A clock strikes four
And I have no idea of time.

Into your arms, I fall . . .

(Translated by Karin Anderson)

Prison

Emmy Hennings

We pull ourselves toward Death with the cord of hope.
Ravens are envious of the prison yards.
Our never-kissed lips quiver.
Powerless solitude, you are magnificent.
The world lies outside there, life roars there.
There men are permitted to go where they like.
Once we also belonged to them.
And now we are forgotten and presumed dead.
At night, we dream of miracles on our plank-beds.
During the days, we move along like frightened animals.
We mournfully look out through the iron railing
And have nothing more to lose
Than the life God gave us.
Only Death lies in our hand.
The freedom no one can take from us:
To go into the unknown land.

(Translated by Mel Gordon)

Dada Manifesto

Tristan Tzara

To launch a manifesto you have to want: A. B. & C., and fulminate against 1, 2, & 3, work yourself up and sharpen your wings to conquer and circulate lower and upper case As, Bs & Cs, sign, shout, swear, organize prose into a form that is absolutely and irrefutably obvious, prove its ne plus ultra and maintain that novelty resembles life in the same way as the latest apparition of a harlot proves the essence of God. His existence had already been proved by the accordion, the landscape and soft words. To impose one's A. B. C. is only natural—and therefore regrettable. Everyone does it in the form of a crystalbluff-madonna, or a monetary system, or pharmaceutical preparations, a naked leg being the invitation to an ardent and sterile Spring. The love of novelty is a pleasant sort of cross, it's evidence of a naive don't-give-a-damn attitude, a passing, positive, sign without rhyme or reason. But this need is out of date, too. By giving art the impetus of supreme simplicity—novelty—we are being human and true in relation to innocent pleasures; impulsive and vibrant in order to crucify boredom. At the lighted crossroads, alert, attentive, lying in wait for years, in the forest. I am writing a manifesto and there's nothing I want, and yet I'm saying certain things, and in principle I am against manifestos, as I am against principles (quantifying measures of the moral value of every phrase—too easy; approximation was invented by the impressionists). I'm writing this manifesto to show that you can perform contrary actions at the same time, in one single, fresh breath; I am against action; as for continual contradiction, and affirmation too, I am neither for nor against them, and I won't explain myself because I hate common sense.

DADA—this is a word that throws up ideas so that they can be shot down; every bourgeois is a little playwright, who invents different subjects and who, instead of situating suitable characters on the level of his own intelligence, like chrysalises on chairs, tries to find causes or objects (according to whichever psychoanalytic method he practices) to give weight to his plot, a talking and self-defining story.

Every spectator is a plotter, if he tries to explain a word (to know!) From his padded refuge of serpentine complications, he allows his instincts to be manipulated. Whence the sorrows of conjugal life.

To be plain: The amusement of redbellies in the mills of empty skulls.

If we consider it futile, and if we don't waste our time over a word that doesn't mean anything . . . The first thought that comes to these minds is of a bacteriological order: at least to discover its etymological, historical or psychological meaning. We read in the papers that the negroes of the Kroo race call the tail of a sacred cow: DADA. A cube, and a mother, in a certain region of Italy, are called: DADA. The word for a hobby-horse, a children's nurse, a double affirmative in Russian and Rumanian, is also: DADA. Some learned journalists see it as an art for babies, other Jesuscallingthelit-tlechildrenuntohim saints see it as a return to an unemotional and noisy primitivism—noisy and monotonous. A sensitivity cannot be built on the basis of a word; every sort of construction converges into a boring sort of perfection, a stagnant idea of a golden swamp, a relative human product. A work of art shouldn't be beauty *per se*, because it is dead; neither gay nor sad, neither light nor dark; it is to rejoice or maltreat individualities to serve them up the cakes of sainted haloes or the sweat of a meandering chase through the atmosphere. A work of art is never beautiful, by decree, objectively, for everyone. Criticism is, therefore, useless; it only exists subjectively, for every individual, and without the slightest general characteristic. Do people imagine they have found the psychic basis common to all humanity? The attempt of Jesus, and the Bible, conceal, under their ample, benevolent wings: shit, animals and days. How can anyone hope to order the chaos that constitutes that infinite, formless variation: man? The principle: "Love thy neighbor" is hypocrisy. "Know thyself" is utopian, but more acceptable because it includes malice. No pity. After the carnage we are left with the hope of a purified humanity. I always speak about myself because I don't want to convince, and I have no right to drag others in my wake, I'm not compelling anyone to follow me, because everyone makes his art in his own way, if he knows anything about the joy that rises like an arrow up to the astral strata, or that which descends into the mines strewn with flowers of corpses and fertile spasms. Stalactites: look everywhere for them, in creches magnified by pain, eyes as white as angels' hares. Thus DADA was born, out of a need for independence, out of mistrust for community. People who join us keep their freedom. We don't accept any theories. We've had enough of the cubist and futurist academies: laboratories of formal ideas. Do we make art in order to earn money and keep the dear bourgeoisie happy? Rhymes have the smack of money, and inflexion slides along the line of the stomach in profile. Every group of artists has ended up at this bank, straddling various comets. Leaving the door open to the possibility of wallowing in comfort and food.

Here we are dropping our anchor in fertile ground.

Here we really know what we are talking about, because we have experienced the trembling and the awakening. Drunk with energy, we are revenants thrusting the trident into heedless flesh. We are streams of curses in the tropical abundance of vertiginous vegetation, resin and rain is our sweat, we bleed and burn with thirst, our blood is strength.

Cubism was born out of a simple manner of looking at objects: Cezanne painted a cup twenty centimeters lower than his eyes, the cubists look at it from above, others complicate its appearance by cutting a vertical section through it and soberly placing it to one side. (I'm not forgetting the creators, nor the seminal reasons of unformed matter that they rendered definitive.) The futurist sees the same cup in movement, a succession of objects side by side, mischievously embellished by a few guide-lines. This doesn't stop the canvas being either a good or a bad painting destined to form an investment for intellectual capital. The new painter creates a world whose elements are also its means, a sober, definitive, irrefutable work. The new artist protests: he no longer paints (symbolic and illusionistic reproduction) but creates directly in stone, wood, iron, tin, rocks, or locomotive structures capable of being spun in all directions by the limpid wind of the momentary sensation. Every pictorial or plastic work is unnecessary, even if it is a monster which terrifies servile minds, and not a sickly-sweet object to adorn the refectories of animals in human garb, those illustrations of the sad fable of humanity.—A painting is the art of making two lines, which have been geometrically observed to be parallel, meet on a canvas, before our eyes, in the reality of a world that has been transposed according to new conditions and possibilities. This world is neither specified nor defined in the work, it belongs, in its innumerable variations, to the spectator. For its creator it has neither cause nor theory. *Order = disorder; ego = non-ego; affirmation = negation:* the supreme radiations of an absolute art. Absolute in the purity of its cosmic and regulated chaos, eternal in that globule that is a second which has no duration, no breath, no light and no control. I appreciate an old work for its novelty. It is only contrast that links us to the past. Writers who like to moralize and discuss or ameliorate psychological bases have, apart from a secret wish to win, a ridiculous knowledge of life, which they have classified, parcelled out, canalized; they are determined to see its categories dance when they beat time. Their readers laugh derisively, but carry on: what's the use?

There is only one kind of literature which never reaches the voracious masses. The work of creative writers, written out of the author's real necessity, and for his own benefit. The awareness of a supreme egoism, wherein laws become insignificant. Every page should explode, either because of its profound gravity, or its vortex, vertigo, newness, eternity, or because of its staggering absurdity, the enthusiasm of its principles, or its typography. On the one hand there is a world tottering in its flight, linked to the resounding tinkle of the infernal gamut; on the other hand, there are: the new men. Uncouth, galloping, riding astride on hiccups. And there is a mutilated world and literary mediacasters in desperate need of amelioration.

I assure you: there is no beginning, and we are not afraid; we aren't sentimental. We are like a raging wind that rips up the clothes of clouds and prayers, we are preparing the great spectacle of disaster, conflagration and decomposition. Preparing to put an end to mourning, and to replace tears by sirens spreading from one continent to another. Clarions of intense joy, bereft of that poisonous sadness. DADA is the mark of abstraction; publicity and business are also poetic elements.

I destroy the drawers of the brain, and those of social organization: to sow demoralization everywhere, and throw heaven's hand into hell, hell's eyes into heaven, to reinstate the fertile wheel of a universal circus in the Powers of reality, and the fantasy of every individual.

A philosophical question: from which angle to start looking at life, god, ideas, or anything else. Everything we look at is false. I don't think the relative result is any more important than the choice of patisserie or cherries for dessert. The way people have of looking hurriedly at things from the opposite point of view, so as to impose their opinions indirectly, is called dialectic, in other words, heads I win and tails you lose, dressed up to look scholarly.

If I shout:

Ideal, Ideal, Ideal

Knowledge, Knowledge, Knowledge,

Boomboom, Boomboom, Boomboom

I have recorded fairly accurately Progress, Law, Morals, and all the other magnificent qualities that various very intelligent people have discussed in so many books in order, finally, to say that even so everyone has danced according to his own personal boomboom, and that he's right about his boomboom: the satisfaction of unhealthy curiosity; private bell-ringing for inexplicable needs; bath; pecuniary difficulties; a stomach with repercussions on to life; the authority of the mystical baton formulated as the grand finale of a phantom orchestra with mute bows, lubricated by philtres with a basis of animal ammonia. With the blue monocle of an angel they have dug out its interior for twenty sous worth of unanimous gratitude. If all of them are right, and if all pills are only Pink, let's try for once not to be right. People think they can explain rationally, by means of thought, what they write. But it's very relative. Thought is a fine thing for philosophy, but it's relative. Psychoanalysis is a dangerous disease, it deadens man's anti-real inclinations and systematizes the bourgeoisie. There is no ultimate Truth. Dialectics is an amusing machine that leads us (in banal fashion) to the opinions which we would have held in any case. Do people really think that, by the meticulous subtlety of logic, they have demonstrated the truth and established the accuracy of their opinions? Even if logic were confirmed by the senses it would still be an organic disease. To this element, philosophers like to add: the power of observation. But this magnificent quality of the mind is precisely the proof of its impotence. People observe, they look at things from one or several points of view, they choose them from amongst the millions that exist. Experience too is the result of chance and of individual abilities. Science revolts me when it becomes a speculative system

and loses its utilitarian character—which is so useless—but is at least individual. I hate slimy objectivity, and harmony, the science that considers
that everything is always in order. Carry on, children, humanity . . .
Science says that we are nature's servants: everything is in order, make both
love and war. Carry on, children, humanity, nice kind bourgeois and virgin
journalists . . . I am against systems; the most acceptable system is that of
having none on no principle. To complete oneself, to perfect oneself in
one's own pettiness to the point of filling the little vase of oneself with
oneself, even the courage to fight for and against thought, all this can suddenly infernally propel us into the mystery of daily bread and the lilies of
the economic field.

What I call the I-don't-give-a-damn attitude of life is when everyone
minds his own business, at the same time as he knows how to respect other
individualities, and even how to stand up for himself, the two-step becoming a national anthem, a junk shop, the wireless (the wire-less telephone)
transmitting Bach fugues, illuminated advertisements and placards for
brothels, the organ broadcasting carnations for God, all this at the same
time, and in real terms, replacing photography and unilateral catechism.

Active simplicity.

The incapacity to distinguish between degrees of light: licking the twilight
and floating in the huge mouth filled with honey and excrement. Measured
against the scale of Eternity, every action is vain—(if we allow thought to
have an adventure whose result would be infinitely grotesque—an important factor in the awareness of human incapacity). But if life is a bad joke,
with neither goal nor initial accouchement, and because we believe we
ought, like clean chrysanthemums, to make the best of a bad bargain, we
have declared that the only basis of understanding is: art. It hasn't the importance that we, old hands at the spiritual, have been lavishing on it for
centuries. Art does nobody any harm, and those who are capable of taking
an interest in it will not only receive caresses, but also a marvelous chance
to people the country of their conversation. Art is a private thing, the artist
makes it for himself; a comprehensible work is the product of a journalist,
and because at this moment I enjoy mixing this monster in oil paints: a
paper tube imitating the metal that you press and automatically squeeze out
hatred, cowardice and villainy. The artist, or the poet, rejoices in the
venom of this mass condensed into one shopwalker of this trade, he is glad
to be insulted, it proves his immutability. The author or the artist praised
by the papers observes that his work has been understood: a miserable lin-
ing to a coat that is of public utility; rags covering brutishness, horse-piss
collaborating with the heat of an animal incubating the baser instincts. Flab-
by, insipid flesh multiplying iself with the aid of typographical microbes.

We have done violence to the snivelling tendencies in our natures. Every
infiltration of this sort is macerated diarrhea. To encourage this sort of art is

to digest it. What we need are strong, straightforward, precise works which will be forever misunderstood. Logic is a complication. Logic is always false. It draws the superficial threads of concepts and words towards illusory conclusions and centers. Its chains kill, an enormous myriapod that asphyxiates independence. If it were married to logic, art would be living in incest, engulfing, swallowing its own tail, which still belongs to its body, fornicating in itself, and temperament would become a nightmare tarred and feathered with protestantism, a monument, a mass of heavy, greyish intestines.

But suppleness, enthusiasm and even the joy of injustice, that little truth that we practice as innocents and that makes us beautiful: we are cunning, and our fingers are malleable and glide like the branches of that insidious and almost liquid plant; this injustice is the indication of our soul, say the cynics. This is also a point of view; but all flowers aren't saints, luckily, and what is divine in us is the awakening of anti-human action. What we are talking about here is a paper flower for the buttonhole of gentlemen who frequent the ball of masked life, the kitchen of grace, our white, lithe or fleshy girl cousins. They make a profit out of what we have selected. The contradiction and unity of opposing poles at the same time may be true. If we are absolutely determined to utter this platitude, the appendix of a libidinous, evil-smelling morality. Morals have an atrophying effect, like every other pestilential product of the intelligence. Being governed by morals and logic has made it impossible for us to be anything other than impassive towards policemen—the cause of slavery—putrid rats with whom the bourgeois are fed up to the teeth, and who have infected the only corridors of clear and clean glass that remained open to artists.

Every man must shout: there is great destructive, negative work to be done. To sweep to clean. The cleanliness of the individual materializes after we ve gone through folly, the aggressive, complete folly of a world left in the hands of bandits who have demolished and destroyed the centuries. With neither aim nor plan, without organization: uncontrollable folly, decomposition. Those who are strong in word or in strength will survive, because they are quick to defend themselves; the agility of their limbs and feelings flames on their faceted flanks.

Morals have given rise to charity and pity, two dumplings that have grown like elephants, planets, which people call good. There is nothing good about them. Goodness is lucid, clear and resolute, and ruthless towards compromise and politics. Morality infuses chocolate into every man's veins. This task is not ordained by a supernatural force, but by a trust of ideas-merchants and academic monopolists. Sentimentality: seeing a group of bored and quarrelling men, they invented the calendar and wisdom as a remedy. By sticking labels on to things, the battle of the philosophers was let loose (money-grubbing, mean and meticulous weights and measures) and one understood once again that pity is a feeling, like diarrhea in relation to disgust, that undermines health, the filthy carrion job of jeopardizing the sun. I proclaim the opposition of all the cosmic faculties to that blennorrhea of a putrid sun that issues from the factories of philosophical thought, the fight to the death, with all the resources of Dadaist disgust.

Every product of disgust that is capable of becoming a negation of the family is *dada*; protest with the fists of one's whole being in destructive action: DADA; acquaintance with all the means hitherto rejected by the sexual prudishness of easy compromise and good manners: DADA; abolition of logic, dance of those who are incapable of creation: DADA; every hierarchy and social equation established for values by our valets: DADA; every object, all objects, feelings and obscurities, every apparition and the precise shock of parallel lines, are means for the battle of: DADA; the abolition of memory: DADA; the abolition of archaeology: DADA the abolition of prophets: DADA; the abolition of the future: DADA; the absolute and indisputable belief in every god that is an immediate product of spontaneity: DADA; the elegant and unprejudiced leap from one harmony to another sphere; the trajectory of a word, a cry, thrown into the air like an acoustic disc; to respect all individualities in their folly of the moment, whether serious, fearful, timid, ardent, vigorous, decided or enthusiastic; to strip one's church of every useless and unwieldy accessory; to spew out like a luminous cascade any offensive or loving thought, or to cherish it—with the lively satisfaction that it's all precisely the same thing—with the same intensity in the bush, which is free of insects for the blue-blooded, and gilded with the bodies of archangels, with one's soul. Liberty: DADA DADA DADA;—the roar of contorted pains, the interweaving of contraries and of all contradictions, freaks and irrelevancies: LIFE.

(Translated by Barbara Wright)

Tristan Tzara

The First Celestial Adventure of Mr. Antipyrine, Fire Extinguisher

Tristan Tzara

MR. BLUEBLUE:
   penetrate the desert
   hollow out your path howling in
   the sticking sand
   listen to the vibration
   the leech and the cocktail-beetle
   maaoi lounda ngami with the hug
   of a child suicide
MR. SHRIEKSHRIEK:
   masks and rotting snows circus
   pskow
   i push factory in the circus pskow
   the sexual organ is square is iron is
   bigger
   than the volcano and flies off
   above mgabati
   offspring of distant mountain
   crevasses
   tropical portugal wharf and
   parthenogenesis
   of long iron hiding things
   dschilolo mgabati bylunda
THE PREGNANT WOMAN:
   toundi-a-voua
   soca bgye affahou
PIPI:
   bitterness without church let's go
   let's git synthetic charcoal camel
   bitterness upon the church
   ururuch the curtains
   dodododo
MR. ANTIPYRINE,
FIRE EXTINGUISHER:
   soco bgye affahou
   zoumbye zoumbye zoumbye
   zoum

MR. SHRIEKSHRIEK:
    there is no humanity there are the
    lamplighters and the dogs
    dzin aha dzin aha bobobo tyao
    cahiiii hii hii
    ayboom
    yeya yeyo
MR. BLUEBLUE:
    incontestably
MR. ANTIPYRINE,
FIRE-EXTINGUISHER:
    door sealed without brotherhood
    we are bitter fel
    twist to cede centipede of the
    eiffel tower
    enlarge lard lord and lard lard
    mechanism without pain
    179858555 yeyo bibo bibi aha
    my god oh my god along the canal
    the fever of childbirth laces and
    SO2H4
MR. BLUEBLUE:
    toubo matapo the viceroys of the
    nights
    they have lost their arms
    mouncangama
    they have lost their arms
    managara
    they have lost their arms irregular
    polygon
    in matzacas the ladybug is bigger
    than the cerebral
    hemisphere
    but where are the houses the
    viceroys of the nights
THE PREGNANT WOMAN:
    four hundred horses sixty camels
    three hundred sable pelts five
    hundred ermine pelts
    her husband is sick
    twenty yellow fox pelts three
    chelizun pelts
    hundred white and yellow

a big bird alive tyao
ty a a ty a o ty a o
MR. SHRIEKSHRIEK:
MR. BLUEBLUE:
PIPI:
MR. ANTIPYRINE,
FIRE-EXTINGUISHER:
zdranga zdranga zdranga zdranga
di di di di di di di di
zoumbye zoumbye zoumbye
zoumbye
dzi dzi dzi dzi dzi dzi dzi dzi
the big one named blueblue
clambers into his despair and
there shits his manifestations from
the last day he wants nothing
from the side and to cloister
himself like the angelus in his
intestinal belfry on the arrival of
the police he is disgusted and gives
up acutely vexed
MR. SHRIEKSHRIEK:
houses flute factory razed head
107 when night came tranquilly
like a scarab
the rabbits surround the cathedral
dral dral and
turn until they become daylight
H2O
like the northerly parties who
surround themselves in
ndjaro
THE DIRECTOR:
he died saying that farce is a
poetic element
like sorrow for example
then they sang
MR. SHRIEKSHRIEK:
THE PREGNANT WOMAN:
PIPI:
MR. ANTIPYRINE,
FIRE-EXTINGUISHER:
crocrocrocrocrocrocrocro

drol
crocrocrocrocrocrocrocro
crodral
in the end he didn't hesitate to
light himself without
help from the cubist and
kintampo and craus and begnius
and nicholas were there and were
canopies the enormous
distances of their enchantment
henceforth called themselves
mganani

PIPI:
i have on my breast 5 so many
beautiful spots
along the edges 16 wounded the
dresses 7 of angels
in a rainbow of center 4

MR. ANTIPYRINE,
FIRE-EXTINGUISHER:
pregnant birds who make number
two on the bourgeois
the doodoo is always a child
the child is always a goose
the doodoo is always a camel
the child is always a goose
and we sing
goo goo goo goo goo goo goo goo
goo goo goo goo goo goo

THE DIRECTOR:
i am historical
you come from martinique
we are very intelligent
and we are not germans

MR. SHRIEKSHRIEK:
the energy of interior movement
quick violin mountain
montenigger balcony
and tomorrow i shall be sick in
the hospital

MR. ANTIPYRINE,
FIRE-EXTINGUISHER:
soco bgye affahou

the quietudes of oil-bearing
swamps
from which watery yellow
swaddling clothes rise at midday
tarafangama the mollusks pedro
ximenez from batumai
puff up the pillows of the birds
Ca2O4SPH
the dilation of the volcanoes soco
bgye affahou
irregular polygon
sick of super sounds and sunshine
MR. BLUEBLUE:
    borkou mmbaz gymnastics
    mmbaz 20785
    under that garbage down there lies
    jerez amantillado
MR. ANTIPYRINE,
FIRE-EXTINGUISHER:
    the narrowest parallelepipeds
    circulate among the microbes
    automobiles and ducks swim in oil
    I want to do justice to you
    erdera vendrell
MR. BANGBANG:
    the songs of the saltimbanques
    reassemble familiarly before
    the departure
    the acrobat secrets spittle in his
    stomach
    to give to grasp among to give to
    give to grasp to grasp
    tigvi tigvge
    iuuuuuuuuuunpht
    there where bird hum 100 sing on
    the page fence
    where night bird sing with the
    archangel
    where night bird sing for apaches
    and you have frozen in heaven
    near my beautiful song
    in a glassware store

NPALA GARROO:
> you roll up the rainbow the clocks
> vaporize
> the navel the sun contracts
> and the student measured his last
> intensity
> he was nevertheless in love and
> croaked

TRISTAN TZARA:
> DADA is our intensity: it sets up
> inconsequential bayonets the
> sumatran head of the german
> baby; Dada is life without slippers
> or parallels; it is against and for
> unity and definitely against the
> future; we know wisely that our
> brains will become downy pillows,
> that our anti-dogmatism is as
> exclusivist as the bureaucrat and
> that we are not free and shriek
> liberty; severe necessity with
> neither discipline nor moral and
> we spit on humanity. DADA
> remains in the european frame of
> weaknesses, it is nevertheless shit,
> but henceforth we want to shit in
> diverse colors to decorate the
> artistic zoo with the flags of every
> consulate. We are circus managers
> and we whistle through the wind
> at the fairs, through the convents,
> brothels, theatres, realities,
> sentiments, restaurants, ohi, hoho,
> bangbang.
> We declare that automobiles are a
> sentiment that have cuddled us
> enough in the slowness of their
> abstractions like ocean liners,
> ruckuses and ideas. Meanwhile we
> exteriorize facility, we search for
> the central essence and we are
> content if we can hide it; we do
> not want to count the windows of

the marvelous elite, for DADA
exists for no one and we want
everyone to understand that. That
is the Dada balcony, I assure you.
From which you can hear the
military marches and come down
slicing the air like a seraphim in a
public bath to piss and understand
the parable.
DADA is neither folly, nor
wisdom, nor irony, look at me
friendly bourgeoisie.
Art was a nut-shell game, the
children assembled words with a
ring at the end, then they cried,
and shrieked the verse, and
decked it out in doll shoes, and
the verse became queen to die a
little and the queen became a
whale and the children all ran till
their breaths did fail.
Then came the great ambassadors
of sentiment who exclaimed
historically in chorus
Psychology Psychology heehee
Science Science Science
Vive la France
We are not naive
We are successive
We are exclusive
We are not simple
and we are all well-versed in
intelligence.
But we, DADA, do not agree with
them, because art is
not serious, I assure you, and if
we show the crime to
say learnedly ventilator, it's to
please you, good
listeners, I love you so much, I
assure you and I adore you.
THE PARABLE:
    if you could ask an old lady
    the address of a bordello

bir bir bir bir bir bir bir bir bird
who sing on the camel's hump
the green elephants of your
sensibility
each one trembling on a telegraph
pole
four feet nailed together
he looked at the sun so much that
his face flattened out
oua aah oua aah oua aah
Mr poet has a new hat
of straw that was so beautiful so
beautiful beautiful
it was like a holy halo
for truly Mr poet was an archangel
that bird came white and feverish
like
from which regiments comes the
clock? from that humid music like
Mr Shriekshriek had a visit from
his fiancee at the hospital in the
jewish cemetary the tombs rise
like serpents
Mr poet was truly an archangel
he said that the druggist was like a
butterfly and like a lord and that
life is simple like a bangbang like
the bangbang of his heart
the woman made from balls in
diminishing sizes began to shriek
like a catastrophe
yes
sssssssssssssssssssssssssssssssssssssssssssss
sssssssssssssssss
the idealist looked at the sun so
much that his face flattened out
taratatatatatatatatata
MR. ANTIPYRINE,
FIRE-EXTINGUISHER:
to ndumba to tritriloulu to
nkogundla
there is a great halo where worms
circulate in silence
for worms and other animals also

have pains
sorrows and inspirations
look at windows that roll up like
giraffes
turn multiply hexagons clamber
tortured
the moon puffs up marsupial and
becomes dog
the macaw and the cockatoo
admire the dog
a lily just bloomed in its asshole
it is the flock of mountains in
shirts in
our church that is the west station
the horses
hanged themselves in bucharest
while looking at mbogo
who got onto their bicycles while
the telegraphic
horses get drunk
some ventriloquist's ears flood
four chimney-sweeps who then
crack up like melons
the photographer-priest delivered
three striped children similar to
the violins on the hill push the
pants a mountebank of lunar
leaves balances himself in his
closet
my beautiful child with glass
breasts with parallel ashen arms,
fix my stomach we must sell the
doll
a naughty boy died somewhere
and we let the brains continue
the mouse runs diagonally across
heaven
the mustard runs from a nearly
squashed brain
we have become lamplighters
lamplighters lamplighters
lamplighters
lamplighters lamplighters

lamplighters
lamplighters lamplighters
lamplighters
and then they went away

(Translated by Ruth Wilson)

BERLIN DADA
1919-20

George Grosz as Dada-Death   Gerhard Preiss as Music-Dada

◦ Berlin Dada, 1919-20

For the most part, the Berlin Dada performances resembled those in Zurich but with greater audience and public interest. Included in this section is *Simply Classical! An Orestia With a Happy Ending*, the puppet play that Walter Mehring wrote for a Dada-Soiree at Max Reinhardt's cabaret, *Schall und Rauch* (December 1919). The play itself is filled with topical references to political, economic, military, and social events that led to the founding of the Weimar Republic. The satirical use of movie clips and a gramophone-chorus reveal early ideas in multi-media staging.

The *Dadafest* by Ben Hecht is a description of the Dada-Soiree of May 24, 1919 that he witnessed as a young newspaperman. *A Visit to the Cabaret Dada* by "Alexis" appeared in *Der Dada* no. 3 and has been variously ascribed to Richard Huelsenbeck and Johannes Baader. It is not clear whether the article is an invented description that was possibly read at a 1919 Dada event in the gallery of Dr. Burchard, or whether it is a partial description of an actual performance there.

Seelen-Automobil (Automobile-Souls) and *Dadatour* by Raoul Haus-mann appeared in Hausmann's book, *Am Angang War Dada*. *The Race Between the Sewing Machine and the Typewriter* was a standard Dada act and is partly described in Hecht's *Dadafest*. Finally, Mehring's manifesto *Conference Mystique in the Esoteric Cabaret* (1920) was given to me by Mehring for translation.

Simply Classical!
An Orestia With a Happy Ending

Walter Mehring
Music by Friedrich Hollaender

CHARACTERS:

1. **Agamemnon in the Bath** (under the pleasing assistance of the original bathtub in the Royal Palace, Berlin)

The Guard, an invalid from the war 1870-71, with a beard a la Emperor
    Wilhelm I
Agamemnon, Royal Highness, commanding general in his best years
Clytemnestra, his wife, bosomy, kallipygose, in critical years, always in a
    morning gown
Aegisthus, her lover, writer and professional moralist
Cass Andra, racy, with lace pants
The Chorus of Newspapermen:
    The gentleman from the conservative newspaper, blond, blue eyes, Teu-
    tonic golden pince-nez;
    The gentleman from the bourgeois newspaper, with a paunch, umbrella
    and eye glasses;
    The gentleman from the social newspaper, clever, diminutive

2. **The Dawn of Democracy**

Aegisthus, democratic president, with Clytemnestra
Clytemnestra
Electra of the Salvation Army
Orestes, officer of an Attic Free Corps, Royal Highness, monocle, Attic Free
    Corps Uniform
The Chorus: a phonograph

3. **The Classic Flight from Taxation**

Henny Pythia, called the Duse of the Nordic Cinema
Woodrow Apollo, unmistakable similarity to President W..., always in
    Yankee clothing, lives only in higher spheres
The Guard, from Act One
Orestes, from Act Two

Chorus:
The Tax Eumenides, formed by the gentlemen from the press, later acting as Supreme Court

Act One

Agamemnon in the Bath

(*A merry black song, brutally interrupted by the loud chords of a reveille. Curtain. The Guard, in full moonlight, with a burning lantern. A gong sounds five times. Flashes of light.*

Hall of columns in the Greek Kurfurstendamm style. Stage right, door to the bedroom; stage left, door with a painted target.

The last sound of the trumpet breaks off croakingly. The Guard, frightened, straightens up, crows, saluting to all sides.)

GUARD:
Good Morning, good morning, good morning!
I'm the guard! At one time
this was rather pleasant.
The artists still had to muse
Over the classicism of clean shoes.
But who today still knows a button stick,
Well, that's the new times.

The girls would lie down before us!
First one went dancing, then behind the bushes—
Today you have to run through twenty places
Get drunk on saccharin and methyl,
And then you still don't get them that far,
Well, that's the new times.

The laurel wreath one gets today second hand
So to speak from the old Empire's stores
Sold underhand at the Alexanderplatz
With all the wigs and costumes.
Twitching with the shoulder, one is informed,
Well, that's the new times.
   (*The doorbell begins to buzz clearly.*)

Now take it easy, there in the early morning
who arrives but the brethren from the press!
If somewhere there lies a cadaver or something is foul in the state
You can be sure that a writer is not far behind.
With His Excellency I only say:
Hands off literature.

(*Pulls out cross-bow or revolver, shoots at the target. The door opens up, bellowing: cuckoo, cuckoo. Guard exits, the journalists enter through the door, in vivid discussion.*)

THE "SOCIAL" GENTLEMAN:
    My colleagues, rightfully we are called
    The Greek chorus in modern garb.
    As reporters we stand above everything
    All opinions leave us cold.
THE "CONSERVATIVE" GENTLEMAN:
    In my honor code it says:
    With God for king and fatherland.
THE "SOCIAL" GENTLEMAN:
    Excuse me, but once I was conservative, too
    But now the social is in the ascendancy.
THE "BOURGEOIS" GENTLEMAN:
    I think it's the artistic mark,
    The ethical content which determines the quota.
THE "SOCIAL" GENTLEMAN:
    In any event, the trash of pomp and beards
    Can only be used stylistically.
    More important than intuition
    Is some solid information
    About what's illegal in court circles.
THE "CONSERVATIVE" GENTLEMAN: (*Angrily.*)
    You know that this falls in my province.
THE "BOURGEOIS" GENTLEMAN:
    Liberalism alone, gentlemen, is of importance
    After all, there is space for all of us in the paper.
    (*Some hearty yeawning is heard through the bedroom door. The chorus of newspapermen immediately takes up its listening posts.*)
A WOMAN'S VOICE: (*Sleepily.*) Well, darling! already awake, my little pig!
THE "CONSERVATIVE" GENTLEMAN: (*Writing.*) That's stuff for a juicy article.
THE "BOURGEOIS" GENTLEMAN: (*Writing.*)
    My poet's wings begin to grow
    For a well-aimed editorial.

A MAN'S VOICE: (*Even more sleepily.*) Let me sleep some more.

THE WOMAN'S VOICE: You're too comfortable. You are becoming like a real husband!

THE MAN'S VOICE: I am not inexhaustible—

THE WOMAN'S VOICE: Fooey! Don't I please you? Look at me.

THE MAN'S VOICE: My child, you have the most exciting naval!

THE "SOCIAL" GENTLEMAN: (*Writing.*) A royal sink of iniquity.

THE WOMAN'S VOICE: Tell me, are you really faithful?

THE MAN'S VOICE:
I can prove it to you.
You are my only liaison in royal circles.
And what is my particular good luck:
Your husband is at the Trojan front.

THE WOMAN'S VOICE: Don't we take a bath today, my love?

THE MAN'S VOICE:
No, no. As aesthetes we are clean anyhow.
In my book: Man is better than good
Cleans the stomach and also the blood.
And the coal crisis . . .

THE WOMAN'S VOICE: You are here among royalty.

THE MAN'S VOICE: Leave me alone with your perversities.

THE "SOCIAL" GENTLEMAN:
Gentlemen, we have a terrific story
And I think, it's enough for today.
We forego cheap relevance
And leave everything else to fantasy.

(*The chorus of the press disappears discreetly behind the other door.*)

THE MAN'S VOICE: (*Screaming.*) Ouch, is that cold! Don't pull the blanket away.

(*Clytemnestra and Aegisthus appear simultaneously at the bedroom door with very red faces, and only partly clothed.*)

CLYTEMNESTRA:
Bring us the bathtub!
(*She then presses Aegisthus against her very cozy bosom, in a sweet voice.*)
Come on, give me a morning kiss!
(*Teasing.*) Or else I will be angry at you.

AEGISTHUS: (*Very cool and gruff.*)
You know, you make me more and more nervous.

In the end I will write to your husband.

(*The telephone at the column rings like crazy.*)

CLYTEMNESTRA: The telephone, the telephone. I have an idea . . .
AEGISTHUS: (*In a rage.*) Women always have ideas.
CLYTEMNESTRA: (*Pulling the receiver.*) Hello . . .
THE TELEPHONE: (*In the most beautiful dark voice.*) Here is Agamemnon.
CLYTEMNESTRA: Who? Wrong connection. This is . . .
AEGISTHUS: (*Runs around, pulling his hair.*)
   I am a moralist, an anti-militarist.
   I am against duels, I cannot stand seeing a fly in rage.
   I cannot look at a uniform or blood.
   That woman has seduced me and now I am done for.
CLYTEMNESTRA: Darling, where shall I hide you in a hurry?
THE TELEPHONE:
   I am coming directly from the trenches
   and look forward to a solemn luncheon!
CLYTEMNESTRA: (*Runs around.*) O, my nerves, I'm losing my mind.
AEGISTHUS: (*Likewise.*)
   This damned telephone
   Spoils my favorite position.
   And now I can start writing poetry again.

(*Horn signals nearing: Ta Tu-ta ta. Clytemnestra and Aegisthus disappear in the bedroom. Agamemnon, spear in hand, and Cass Andra enter simultaneously.*)

AGAMEMNON:
   Well, Cass Andra, you smart ass
   Tell me how you like it here.
CASS ANDRA:
   Well, fatso, first give me the powder
   Before you introduce me to your wife,
   And, after all, I don't care much
   I can see this any day in our glass house
   And I am not impressed by any movie.
AGAMEMNON: But you can show some better manners.

(*Honking, a steamer arrives.*)

CASS ANDRA: Well, well . . .
AGAMEMNON:
   Well, you see, now you are surprised,

This is no steamboat, it is a bathtub
Which a colleague of mine in Berlin
has lent me from his royal castle.
He has now dissolved his household.
But it all has to be seen symbolically:
Once you are dry and then again you are wet
And our future lies in the water.

CASS ANDRA: Well, let's have fun. (*They throw off their clothes, she stands in undies, he in trunks. The door with the target calls "cuckoo" and opens, a reporter's head becomes visible.*)

AGAMEMNON:

What the heck! The press has to
poke its nose into everything.
If you need them, they aren't around
And when you don't, they watch you!

CASS ANDRA: (*With a tender embrace.*)

Why don't you relax in the tub,
Good publicity can never hurt.

(*Together they climb into the overflowing bath shower, singing.*)

CASS ANDRA & AGAMEMNON:

If only Aeschylus were to know
With happiness he would overflow
A bit of classicism in a modern way
Redoubles the humor, he would say.

In school we already learn Greek
And students think it is quite chic
To see such an old Greek gent
Exposing himself indecent.

If only Aeschylus . . .

Go to Reinhardt when he curses,
It is classic how he rehearses.
Smoothly runs the Orestia
All with his machinery.

If only Aeschylus . . .

(*The reporters run pell-mell across the stage, camera in hand, to shoot the bathing scene.*)

THE "CONSERVATIVE" GENTLEMAN:
    Bravo, a highly risky posture,
    Every inch a king of trunks!
THE "BOURGEOIS" GENTLEMAN:
    Miss Andra, look sweetly up to me,
    Your smile is worth its weight in gold.
THE "SOCIAL" GENTLEMAN:
    One likes the truth now when it's naked
    This will make the most fascinating bathroom scene
    And fits into the royal series well.
CASS ANDRA: Display my name as large as possible, will you? (*The "social" gentleman mistakenly exits into the bedroom. Clytemnestra appears. Cass Andra shrieks.*) Wow, the wife! (*Clytemnestra immediately grasps the situation, with hysterical pathos.*)
CLYTEMNESTRA:
    For heaven's sake,
    This is a true sex film,
    Like a picture by Grosz, shameless, free-and-easy.

(*The steamboat stops amidst painful honking and puffing. Agamemnon and Cass Andra stand trembling and wet.*)

AGAMEMNON:
    I'm getting the flu, throw me a hankie fast
    I feel like a misplaced Othello.

(*Aegisthus appears, as in a frame-up, with waving arms.*)

AEGISTHUS:
    The performance will be stopped.
    Allow me, Miss, to confiscate you.
CLYTEMNESTRA: (*Energetically separating Aegisthus from Cass Andra.*)
    In this house I am the director,
    You, Miss, disappear among the extras.
CASS ANDRA: (*In a dashing voice.*)
    For me this is all the best possible publicity
    The more you scream and puff.
CLYTEMNESTRA: (*Pulls Aegisthus to her in the steamer.*)
    Come, sweetie, we shall manage now.
    (*They depart with loud honking.*)
AEGISTHUS: (*Bellows.*)
    Morality wins!
CASS ANDRA: Curtain, curtain! Dim the lights, dim the lights!

AGAMEMNON: (*His rigidity is dissolved by heavy sneezing.*) Thank God.
CASS ANDRA: (*Hugging him.*)
Fatso, you'll make a marvelous king
For my Cass Andra Movie, Inc.

Act Two

The Dawn of Democracy

(*A bedroom. In the rear wall a comfortable toilet.*)

AEGISTHUS: (*In a morning gown, practicing in sweat at the punching ball.*)
Ladies and gentlemen! It's easy to laugh!
But do better! Do better than that.
After all, have you ever ruled a country?
(*Begins throwing some hard punches.*)
Sometimes they stab you on the Left, and sometimes on the Right.
Sometimes they bloody you in the morning papers.
Or caricatured by Zille—
You are searched, ridiculed, spied upon.
There is no romanticism to it anymore,
No heroic posture, no gigantic iambics.
There are no more crowns, no more kingly ways.
In one word: it no longer pays.
If your name is Werfel or Romain Rolland,
It's certain that no cat will bite.
But embrace the intellectuals into peace and quiet,
The Dada-rebels will begin their riots.
No longer will I look stupid,
Swallowing Mondamin and cocaine,
Gotta do daily several hours of gymnastics,
Make "my system" fit and sane.
Until in the end you sadly feel
There is no love in the human race.

(*Electra of the Salvation Army slowly crosses the stage with a phonograph playing the beautiful song: "It's dawn, it's dawn." Aegisthus goes down on all four and stares into the phonograph's funnel.*)

AEGISTHUS:
Who is coming there? If I see correctly,
She is Electra of the Salvation Army.

Well, Miss, first of all you disturb
The deepest peace of democracy.
And then you are no longer allowed to walk back and forth,
For disarmament also holds for the heavenly hosts.
ELECTRA:
Unfortunately the currency of faith is falling,
Ending in the catastrophe of a church boycott.
I collect money for starving Anti-semites.
AEGISTHUS:
You must offer something better.
What about a modern foxtrot?
ELECTRA:
Sir, I serve here only one God.
And, on the side, I deal with machines
With which cultured nations can toast Jews,
    (*Smelling a rat, she continues in her more familiar Berlin dialect.*)
And for you, you silly fool
I will not start anything new.
If you think you can make fun of me,
I shall get my brother.
ORESTES: (*In each hand a poison gas grenade.*)
This is going to be handled painlessly,
The guy is a democrat, he can't give satisfaction.
    (*Screaming.*)
I'm holding a grudge against you for a long time, you wise guy.
You liberal peace lover.
I'm here to put things in order.
AEGISTHUS: (*Withdrawing.*)
Do not wave with those weapons, please.
Too easy for them to explode.
ORESTES: (*Attacking.*)
You are already known from Ae . . . Aeschylus
All of that classical riff-raff,
That liberal education humbug
Our youth must now learn instead of making war.
That must be radically changed
AEGISTHUS:
Help, help, help!
For being a martyr I have not the slightest talent
I am nothing but a simple president.
ORESTES: Such literary infected bloating.

(*Aegisthus saves himself by going to the toilet where the water rushes.*)

AEGISTHUS: My kingdom for a biplane now.

(Orestes throws the hand grenade: explosion, accompanied by awful noise. Aegisthus disappears in the toilet. Clytemnestra bursts despairingly into the room.)

CLYTEMNESTRA:
    Good heavens, where are you, Aegisthe, Aegisthe?
    I believe that he, who rages here, is a Bolsheviste.
    My God, what do I see, it's my son.
ORESTES:
    I can't stand that Hasenclever jargon.
    Mom, you behave not at all in style.
    You pushed my old man unceremoniously
    And without a sufficient pension
    From his throne, and therefore . . .
        (He swings the second hand grenade, Clytemnestra falls down. Orestes
        walks towards the body, saluting.)
    You see, it works this way too
    And style is observed.
    Even in the most painful situation
    Good taste is indeed preserved. *(Exit.)*

(Pink light. The toilet washes Aegisthus's body overboard. Electra appears. The phonograph plays: "It is dawn, it is dawn.")

FILMIC INTERLUDE

HENNY:
    I am the Duse
    Without the fuse.
    Gas is scarce but my star shines.
    I smile for a minister's wages.
    If Gretchen I play,
    Each girl will say:
    "If only I were Henny!" How does she do it?
    If only I knew how.
    Therefore I wrote a book, containing what I had to say,
    How I became what I am today.

    Is there a crisis, then
    At the top suddenly appears a new man.
    They criticize him Left and Right,

And if it becomes tight
Totally failing he might.
From everywhere it sounds: What the hell is he doing?
He doesn't know how the political game is going.
Therefore he wrote a book, containing what he had to say:
How I became what I am today.

Wherever they play
Films, theatre or baccarat
Everywhere Mr. Lehmann is to be seen,
Formerly he dealt with herrings.
But no one can get a glance of his books.
Damn it, the guy, what is he doing?
He really knows how the game is going.
But in his book, he had nothing to say
About how he became what he is today.
(*Making a bow, tremendous applause, exit.*)

Act Three

The Classic Flight from Taxation

(*Two frontier posts. A poster with the words: "Millionaires must use the field path." A popular hit melody is played. The Tax Eumenides, formerly the chorus of the press, appear, tapping. Orestes, carrying several bags, appears. The Eumenides stiffen to attention.*)

ORESTES:
    Stop that asinine jumping around.
    When I come, you should sing Hallelujah.
    Here I stand, heavily loaded down.
    Nobody makes a speech and there are no flags.
    If one crosses the frontier, this requires
    At least several farewell wreaths.
THE EUMENIDES: (*All three moving in the same way.*)
    Beg your pardon, Your Highness, ours is the duty
    To patrol here as tax eumenides.
    That not all the money goes abroad.
    Millionaires must use the field road.
ORESTES:
    I have with me nothing but a few paltry millions
    And my Browning with some munition.

My moneys which were in real estate
And a bag full of military effects.
Well, I don't care about some bullions of silver. (*Grabs.*)
THE EUMENIDES: (*Conciliatory.*)
If Your Highness intends to take off—
We don't care. We are not looking.
If Your Highness will only take the field road.
ORESTES:
I've said it once before,
I am in no mood for trifling and for questions.
As a military man I always go straight ahead,
And as for taxes—you wouldn't expect me to.

(*Woodrow Apollo floats on stage as a kind of higher power and speaks from the air.*)

WOODROW APOLLO:
Beg your pardon, as I was just notified by wireless
Your Highness intends to go abroad a bit
I am coming about the fourteen points.
ORESTES: With you there seems to be a propeller loose.
WOODROW APOLLO:
Oh, Highness, you are a bit of a wag
But so congenial as a money maker.
The case, however, is quite complicated.
I have studied international law,
According to which you as a king are inviolable.
ORESTES:
Well, I find this quite hilarious.
Seems you want to fish in troubled waters.
Always desirous to interfere from above.
Putting on the air of God-given destiny,
It is as if one were watching a bad movie.
And for your international law I do not care a bit.
THE EUMENIDES:
If Your Highness will humbly allow,
We'll take care of the matter right away.
ORESTES: I thought you represent the tax authority?
THE EUMENIDES:
We do everything. First we were just the press,
Dance and play on behalf of the people's interests.
Now we have staged a state court.
Just a moment, your Highness. You'll see, your Highness.

*(The Eumenides, Orestes and the floating Woodrow Apollo exit, danc-
ing and singing lustily.)*

You box and foxtrot and pass the difficult times in revelry
And if you still work, I feel sorry for you.
The best of all state bonds
Is of use only to the paperhanger
And we are bankrupt either way.

*(Henny Pythia skips once more onto the stage and begins with her old
song.)*

HENNY PYTHIA:
    I am like the Duse
    Play everything in original costumes
    On the top a crown
    But with nothing further down
    And I smell from the perfume of innocence.

*(There are shouts: "Stop it," "Bravo," "Shocking." The Eumenides and
gentlemen of the press, solemn in their official robes, assemble. Orestes
comes, catches sight of Pythia.)*

ORESTES:
    Good gracious, I like that girl.
    Pretty well developed for her age.
    Miss, you can stay here for a while
    I only have to attend to one matter.

(The State Court opens its session.)

THE "CONSERVATIVE" GENTLEMAN: *(Now president, reads off the
    particulars.)* Mr. Defendant, your Highness Orestes from Mycena,
    Dionysic, of Hellenic nationality.
THE GUARD: *(From Act One, appears, out of breath, reports.)*
    Mr. Woodrow Apollo let you know,
    He cannot come. He leaves it all to the government.
ORESTES:
    Then I will take over the leadership.
    You all need some military discipline,
    Guts in your bones and also more dash.
    Look only how your caps
    Sit sloppily on your heads.

(Steps out to straighten the caps.)
That's already better. Attention, right turn.
Guard, you command: Forward to the Baltic states!

(Orestes and Pythia exeunt, followed by the three-member court.)

ORESTES AND PYTHIA: *(Sing as a farewell.)*
If only Aeschylus were to know . . .

(A brass band intones the March of the Toreador.)

CURTAIN

(Translated by Henry Marx)

Dadafest

Ben Hecht

It was a large concert hall. Huge, excitingly painted posters advertising the Great Art Festival had signaled for weeks from hundreds of Berlin walls and fences. The posters proclaimed the FIRST GERMAN POST-WAR RENAISSANCE OF THE ARTS. ADMISSION, 20 GOLD MARKS. FORMAL DRESS REQUIRED.

I sat in my box and looked down on an audience of Berlin's most distinguished citizens in their finest military and civilian plumage.

The ornate assemblage of culture lovers looked patiently on the brightly lighted, bare stage. A figure in a frock coat and a yellow straw hat walked onto the stage.

I didn't recognize Grosz for several minutes, because he spoke in German and was in blackface.

Another man in a dress suit appeared, carrying a cello. He sat down on a kitchen chair and started tuning his instrument. During the tuning Grosz executed what he fancied was a Negro jig. The tuning over, both performers exited. There was no applause.

My tall friend, Dr. Doehman, appeared next, in tails and opera hat. He held up a hand for silence and then cried out the motif for the evening. I knew enough German by that time to make it out.

"Art is in danger!" Dr. Doehman announced.

The black-face Grosz rushed from the wings and roared at the audience another warning:

"Take your foot out of the butter before it is too late."

A series of acts followed. Grosz, Doehman, and Tautz, up from Munich for the Art Festival, did the announcing. I remember a few of them. There was a race between a girl at a sewing machine and a girl at a typewriter. Grosz fired a starting gun. The girls began sewing and typewriting at top speed. The sewing machine operator was pronounced the winner. She received a set of false whiskers, and went off the stage, proudly wearing them. There was no applause.

The first "Pan-Germanic Poetry Contest" followed. Eleven seedy-looking fellows shuffled out on the stage. They wore large ribbon badges with their entry numbers on them. Several of them were barefoot. They were introduced by Doehman as Germany's leading poets. A twelfth figure appeared and was identified as a *gepacktraeger* (a baggage smasher). He and the eleven poets were to compete for a grand prize.

Grosz appeared and fired his starter's gun. The eleven poets and the red cap began to recite their twelve different poems, simultaneously, at the top of their voices. They made gestures, brushed tears from their eyes, held hands over their hearts.

At the height of the impassioned static from the poets, Grosz fired his gun as a finishing signal. Dr. Doehman strode onto the stage and announced the contest was a draw. The cellist appeared, sat down, and started tuning his instrument, again. Grosz repeated his jig.

There was also a "Recital for the Eye of Modern Music." This event had been specially advertised in the festival posters: BEETHOVEN, BACH ARE DEAD—BUT MUSIC MARCHES ON.

Three girls in tights appeared. They placed a dozen large canvases, one by one, on an easel. Each canvas contained the drawing of a single musical note.

Grosz joined me in my box.

"It is a great success, is it not," he said, trying to speak in Negro dialect . . . . "I am very happy tonight. I have fallen in love with an exceedingly fine young lady, the one who put F sharp on exhibition. She is a typist. It was her first appearance in tights, that is, to an audience. In private she undresses the same as all women do, of every age. But it is not her nudity I am in love with, but her name. Her name is Eva."

Grosz darted off. The Dadaist battle-cries of art in danger and a foot too long in the butter began rising from different parts of the concert hall.

Finally, the audience started its counterrevolution. Officers drew guns and fired at the stage. Police and soldiery appeared. High officers demanded the arrest of the hooligans who had swindled and mocked Berlin's elite. But there was no one to arrest. The Dadaists had melted into the spring night.

The Race Between the Sewing Machine and the Typewriter

George Grosz & Walter Mehring

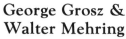

Walter Mehring,
the Featherweight.

MASTER OF CEREMONIES: (*To the Sewing Machine.*) Böff, World Champion in Procreation and Perforation of Culture! (*To the Typewriter.*) Walt Merin, Featherweight!

BÖFF: "Schnurre,schnurre— basselurre."

WALT: Tacktacktack! Bumsti! Ping, ping!

BÖFF: (*Solo on the okarina.*) Tülitetüt, lüttitüt! O sole mio! Old man's river; Mississippi . . .

WALT: . . . et Rataplan, rataplan!

BÖFF: Wille, wille. Wau, wau!

WALT: (*In an aside.*) . . . by Wolfgang Goethe!

BÖFF & WALT: (*In unison.*) Eiapopeia! Tandaradei! Hipp, hipp Dada . . .Dada-capo!

(Translated by Mel Gordon)

George Grosz, Böff,
the World Champion.

A Visit to the Cabaret Dada

"Alexis"

I perform
this
for no
stairways
but
for
a
FORK.
John
Heartfield

Gentlemen, the spectacle begins before you can possibly know it! We walked down a long corridor, each holding a candle with the ladies in front and the men in the rear. The leader, dressed in a white fur coat with a *mitra* on his head, called out several times: "Lift your hands up high and let your belly fall. Grab the kettledrum in your ear and pull the coffin out of your nose—for who knows what good they are?" Then he slammed his earhorn against the wall causing the limestone to break and fall. Yet we felt constantly ill at ease when his voice rang out. Uncertainty rested heavily upon our breasts and upon Councilman Spätzle, a well-known member of the German National Socialist Party. We all began to sink to our knees, although Councilman Spätzle attempted to hold himself erect as long as humanly possibly by means of his moral turpitude. We walked for more than two hours through this corridor that stank of coal and garbage . . . climbing over railroad ties, wooden blocks, and rotten mattresses and eventually found ourselves in a room evidently destined for ecclesiastical purposes . . . There stood the first Dada priest whom I have ever seen, dressed in violet underpants, holding a cat. On his head, he wore a great wig in which two peacock feathers were struck. When he spoke, handfuls of teeth fell from his mouth, and in his ears pinwheels rotated to the clash of military music. . . . The floor shifted so many times and proved to be so slanted that many of the guests fell down, causing some of the women a good deal of anxiety—least the sight of their legs turn the liberal men's attention away from the ceremony. Steam came pouring out through a crack in the masonry, and jets of hot water brust forth from the corners. (Ladies and gentlemen—it was simply overwhelming!) The priest lifted a papier-mache bust and manipulated the eyes, which he controlled by means of a string, to flash back and forth. His voice was like the thunder that ascends from watering cans when the evening sun shines on them. He had a beard in which little mice squeaked "good night," and the express trains were waiting on the abyss of his neck. "I am the priest," he said, "fron the beginning until the end. I am the tulip of Valparaiso and the butterchurn from the Bismark-Archipelago." In our party, the voices of those who saw through this swindle grew; they wanted nothing more than to return to their norm of peace and quiet. "We need work and an organized reconstruction of the fatherland," said a gentleman next to me, who later prospered as a very radical politician . . ." We want our money, we want our money back," shouted a woman with a throaty delivery. In general, the consensus was that one could have spent a more profitable evening reading a good book, worshipping Goethe, or drinking beer—in short, by promoting German culture. Meanwhile, the priest had sat down on his right side, pulled a rabbit out of his toes, and said, "I am the young moon which stands on the waterfall. When I laugh, the earth goes out, and the houses, which stand so rigid knowing nothing, reassemble themselves on the Kaiser-Friedrich Platz. Hail! Hail! The heavens burst, the flute splits apart. Still, morning is not all darkness nor even the equinox of the travel bureau." The man next to me said, "You may not believe it, but behind Dadaism stands the scantiest intelligence. These men are only craft frauds, who know very well that the people are enticed by the irrational; and in that cunning manner, they pull the money from the people's pockets. Look there! That guy is laughing so hard that the tears are rolling down his cheeks." Just then a young woman became indignant. "He isn't laughing," her voice a falsetto, "that is truly enrapture! I've seen the Dadas in Dresden, when chairs were broken over their bodies and pianos shot at their heads. What we call courage is Dada!" The priest in his violet underpants began to roll around on the floor. A moving sidewalk brought in the prima donna from the Metropolitan Opera House, who knew how to whistle the ragtime song, "La délice," on one leg. One could hardly look at the leg without becoming flushed with emotion. The sea cows came very close, perhaps when they wanted to eat out of our hands, and the huge green lizard that hung on the ceiling began to spin like a fan. Everyone talked about the hothouse atmosphere and the ventriloquist-voice about which Capasses has so many significant words to say in his famous novel, *Chevilles*. I did not notice it but Councilman Spätzle was growing into a tremendous rage. "What," he screamed. "What? How dare this be offered to me! Me, who was born of respectable parents, who had a good primary education, who took nine years of classes at a liberal arts *gymnasium*. I have always been in favor of progress. However, what is too much, is too much." He looked around. "And from a nationalistic point of view (he laughed sarcastically) these Dadas are only opposed to the Entente in order to make revolution. Look at him, (the Dadasoph had suddenly appeared) is he a man or an animal?" A heated discussion ensued as to whether the Dadasoph who had just come

Where can you spend Eternity?
At Dr. Otto Burchard's Dada-Soirees.

up out of a trap-door was a man or an animal. The latter was decided upon. No sooner had the Councilman grown silent than a great procession of Dada-like Last Judgments began. It was as if the building would collapse upon our heads. On an immense sofa, they brought in the so-called President of the Universe, Johannes Baader, formerly a tailor who was provided with the necessary accoutrements to distinguish him as a madman and Dionysian dullard. Hot water flowed by the gallons from his ears, and on the seat of his pants he had sewn boxing gloves, on which should have been inscribed the motto of his eternal enterprise: "The Beloved Life of Dadaism." On either side of him stood the Dadasoph Hausmann and Huelsenbeck, who, it is said, is the creator of this nonsense. The Dadasoph rode on an owl, the beast of wisdom, and carried in his hand the symbol of Zarathustra, the serpent and the eagle. "The world as a problem of knowledge," he said, "is Taboo-Dada. From the Eternal One we came to the pigs. Hopsassa!" At these words, a gentleman in our company, who with great difficulty had read Hegel and Schopenhauer, became agitated. The Propaganda-Marshal Grosz appeared with a kettledrum—that symbol of Dada world domination. Close behind him followed the well-known Dada Minister of Commerce and Monteurdada Heartfield. It was an impressive assemblage. An endless procession joined in. The Dadas of all leading countries followed on the backs of cows and horses or on foot. They carried toy trumpets and rattles, and all of them were characterized by the same facial expressions. The troubadour and epicurean of the Paris movement, Herr Tristan Tzara, was there in the uniform of a subway employee. Kurt Schwitters, the world famous author of *Anna Blume*, was seen at a distance. The din was so great that our eardrums cried like little children. Great soft bones fell from the ceiling. (No one knew what purpose that served.) Then the tailor Baader screamed, "Dada is the victory of cosmic intelligence over the Demi-urgos. Dada is the Cabaret of the world, just as the world is Cabaret Dada. Dada is God, Spirit, Matter, and roast veal at the same time." The man next to me yelled in a rage. "Dada," he said, "is planned nonsense. Dada means the end of the German elementary school and the destruction of the German soul!" I joined in the argument and left the Cabaret with him the very same way from which we had come . . . .

(Translated by Mel Gordon)

The ration card for bread this week carries the caption: ARP-like crust

SEELEN-AUTOMOBIL
Solao Solaan Alamt
lanee leneao amamb
ambi ambee enebemp
enepao kalopoo senou
seneakpooo sanakoumt
saddabt kadou koorou
lapidakal adathoum
adaneop ealop noamth.
Raoul Hausmann.

Dadatour

Raoul Hausmann

In January 1920, I had found out by accident that the Oberdada Baader had concluded an agreement with the concert director Schönfelder to perform a solo Dada-Soiree.

I ran immediately to Huelsenbeck and explained the situation.

That night we set off for Dresden. Our first words there being: "What are you looking at with such inflamed eyes, dear Baader? The Weltdada and the Dadasoph are here to help you with your soiree."

Dresden was full of intellectuals and other idiots. Therefore, I knew that something had to happen. So I borrowed a giant gramophone from a music shop and bought several dozen firecrackers in a drug store.

When the evening in the Grain Exchange hall began, I carried a green sofa onto the stage past the idling stagehands, "because," as I told Huelsenbeck, "as soon as we sit down, Baader will introduce us."

The stage was surrounded by a huge green velvet curtain, through whose slit I shoved the gramophone horn and began to play some glorious jazz-music.

Behind the curtain we heard the roar of the crowd. From time to time I tossed a couple of firecrackers to the stage.

Exactly at eight p.m., we entered the hall, proceeding to our sofa, smoking cigarettes, and looked with astonishment at the howling crowd that was threateningly close to us and extended all the way back to the rear window of the hall.

I shouted to Huelsenbeck: "Would you just look at this big crock of shit before us!"

A horrifying roar was the response.

Then Baader introduced us.

Huelsenbeck stood up and delivered a Dada-speech, during which someone bellowed from a window: "Listen, you write that the cows are sitting on the telegraph wires, playing chess. What's the meaning of that?"

Huelsenbeck sat down.

My turn was next.

I read from a manuscript, *The Dada Revenge*, among others: "Let me assure you that you have only your Generals Hindendorf and Lundenburg to thank for your pitiful lives: They are sentencing you to death! And your German poets from Goethe to Werfel, from Schiller to Hasenclever deserve to be flushed down the toilet!"

That was the last straw.

The audience screamed, "Hang them! Skin them! Beat them to death! They're only Communists who've taken our money!"

A couple of dozen men scampered up on the stage and attacked us. I was pushed off the edge of the stage to the floor, where a number of people trampled over me. My pants were ripped and my glasses broken.

I screamed, "Leave me alone. I'm a foreigner."

When I returned to the stage platform, I saw how Huelsenbeck and Baader had defended themselves.

As we soon discovered, the group of young people who were attacking us were from the Socialist Youth League. Once we protested that we were "one with them," they let us off.

Then I shouted to the crowd, "This fighting for us was only a pleasant massage—but for you, a total disgrace! Now, we will set up a discussion session. One speech for every man in the audience. Three minutes speaking time each. Go!"

The first speaker was already there—but no Dada. He went right into "To the gallows with them. Give us our money back!"

Frenzy in the hall.

After this scene repeated itself five or six times, I pleaded with Baader "You must save us. Give them a song and dance."

Baader got up and assured the wild horde that we were against the cinema and the circus. He spoke for about five minutes and managed to bring about some calm.

Then we experienced a little joy: the poet Baron von Lücken had climbed up on the stage and shouted back to the audience, "I find Dada wonderful, and this has been a very lovely evening! Therefore, I will now donate to the Dadas all the money that I have on me—five Marks."

Meanwhile, the proprietor had telephoned the police since it didn't seem as if the commotion would ever die down, and a few armchairs were already destroyed. The police just stuck their heads in the doorway and said, "Ach, it's only the Dadas" and departed.

Since this Dada could no more be Superdada, we tried to get our coats, but the cloakroom was locked.

I divided Baron von Lücken's five Marks with the stagehands whereupon we received our coats and were led out through a back entrance because the crowd was waiting for us at the main entrance in order to settle a few remaining accounts.

(Translated by Mel Gordon)

Conference Mystique in the Esoteric Cabaret

Walter Mehring

"Ladies and Gentlemen! The cabaret is in vogue!"

They call to us, these people who have come out of the pits of Hell—fully cultivated. And we are not suprised that from their superior intelligence we will be presented with something awesome. And for this special goal, no language is as shrill as theirs; no language (even in dialect) is as garbled as this one. But also no type of stanza is so utterly absurd as the chanson, the song, the couplet; and for this very reason there is nothing that is as full of secret possibilities as the language of the cabaret.

Rhyme, as you know, belongs to the abnormal, the strange: A pathological hyperaesthetic, a manifestation of decadence that deranges the nervous system. When children are overcome by frenzy while singing the Gospel, they are really "speaking in tongues"—one of the primary acts of the Byzantine cabaret.

That melancholy decline—the refrain—even now shows us the form of paranoia. One imagines that there is in good society a fine gentleman who, toward every fifth sentence, repeats:

Ride with us to Rügenwalde
On our mini-train,
And you'll feel the evening air
As soft as an animal's mane.

Already the ambulance stands before the door, and the madman continues to wash his sheepskin in innocence. For respect whistles before the guns of irrationality. Later, when the holy shithouses have been made accessible to everyone, the Veil of the Immaculate Conception will have fallen. Ladies and Gentlemen! Your liaison with the beautiful arts (foremost with that of the cabaret) is one of filth. Cleanse it!

Literature for the bourgeois is only a string of facts, from which the pro- fundity of his own thoughts begins to dazzle him. But he wants to be tickled when he sees the well-advertised men and women drunkenly gesturing on the podium. He wants to laugh like the Devil because someone on stage throws a fit of epilepsy every time he hears the theme from *Csardas*. The dirty joke, otherwise only whispered at one's private table, rings in the bourgeois' ears with the clanging of drums and trumpets or to the vibrating sounds of organs.

This is the curse of the culturally lost! For the bourgeois is, in reality, the greatest despiser of tradition. He doesn't know or doesn't want to know that the smile of the circus clown grows out of the *ecco homo* spirit of the Passion Play. Chanson with refrains were the invention of the early Christians, from which the Apocryphal texts were first derived. Eventually, all that remains is the litany and the puppet-song.

The cabaret's infernal pendant, the variety show, developed in a similar manner. In the Middle Ages, only the people with the most horribly distorted bodies were allowed to carry on the "business." The lips of children were torn and their noses sliced off so that they would be guaranteed an artistic career. The clowns and eccentric actors of today are guided by that very principle, only that they awaken the same reaction in the audience with rouge. Their exaggerated movements satirize the crippled and the hysterical.

The cabaret-theatre-art connoisseur anticipates this analogy in the productions by those with abnormally developed minds or astral bodies. He places the entertainer with the possessed and the criminally insane. But only an ethically confused epoch allows itself to palm off army parades as the processions of flagellants and cabaret as the Black Mass. Although the problem is oft-cited, we must again consider the realities: we are not permitted to speak of the Bacchic rites because they are called *Table d'hôte* nor of orgies when we "go into the beautiful evening!" We only do "as if!"

But even the "as if" is not intensive enough! A patented reality masks itself through illusionism. The exploitation of our time would not be so bad, except that it urges everything toward cowardice. And the theatrical performances in the main are not so mediocre as standardless! Kitsch! Yet beastliness and patriotism in themselves are not offensive; they must however first be grafted and pruned in an intellecutal hothouse atmosphere. For only sexual perversity brings out the objectionable.

But my new cabaret is an esoteric one. Only for the initiated! One must start at the beginning of the initiation or buy his way up. Of course, it is not necessary to swerve from the classical forms—there are a thousand drums but only two have sing-song quality (the erotic: "Violets with Garlic Sauce" and the patriotic: "Promises with Lye." In this, they resemble the Taylor System in art: the smallest display of sentiments produces the greatest glandular change in the audience).

Now, with the words on the programs and wine-lists that you will find when you arrive:

I will with other tongues
And with different lips speak to these people,
And they will hear me not!
(*1 Cor. 14*)

I will inaugurate the sequence of the esoteric cabaret. It reads:

1) Overture of the opera *The Ten Sephirot*
2) W. M.: Conference mystique
3) Anna Pohl: Chansons in the style of the *fleur du mal*
4) Blandine Ebinger: Couplets à la *Gil de Rais*
5) *Danse macabre* of the hundred Gibson Girls
6) Friedrich Hollaender: a) Tango harikiri
   b) the amok-runner two-step
7) Giampietro: "In Seventh Heaven" (a divine couplet)
8) *The Urinanalysis*—a sketch
Characters: A gonococcus germ, the wurst-slicer, the hermaphrodite with eyeglasses and a divining rod.

SELA!

(Translated by Mel Gordon)

DADA IN COLOGNE AND HANOVER 1918-23

Drawing by
Kurt
Schwitters
of his
MERZ-Stage

Dada in Cologne and Hanover, 1918-23

Few of the performance activities of the German Dadas outside Berlin were reported in newspaper accounts. Therefore it is difficult to assign any of their dramatic or play-like texts to a production context and history. Some of them might have been performed in a staged-reading situation. Johannes Baargeld's *Bulletin D* falls into this terrain. Originally it was published in his journal *Bulletin D* (Cologne, 1919).

Kurt Schwitters's manifesto "To All the Theatres of the World I Demand the Merz-Stage" appeared in several versions in 1919. The one published here is from his 1919 book *Anna Blume*. The four Schwitters playlets are from 1919, 1922 and 1923. How these were actually performed is not clear.

Bulletin D

... knocks the warm egg out of the hand!

Johannes Theodor Baargeld

AHEHE: Cezanne is chewing gum. The Grunewald digests van Gogh's yellow denture. Van Gogh had an offensive breath and is dead. Eljen dada!

BEHEHE: The Phallustrade of the expressionists exhausts the lecithin store of the whole built-up and known stomach crust. The abdominal bandage of Patti has been buried. Dr. Rudolf Steiner's coroners joined the international DADA Association (iadede). Eviva dada!

CEHEHE: oncasso cassa picasso. Citizen Pablo Picasso distributes his finished oeuvre to Madrid's widows. Now the widows are able to take a course in Swedish massage in order to . . . . picasso Umdada?

DEHEHE: The tooth counselor (?) was a woman. Expressionism is a skin bandage of umbilical cord character. Report: Conjunctiva ok.

EHEHE: Therefore Professor Oskar Kokoschka can now with certainty be considered the inventor of the automechanical leech "Selfhelp." Et Propopo, et Propopos!

FEHEHE: Hasenclever in white tennis shorts! Hasenclevers, unite! Da, ut dem dada.

GEHEHE: Art grows on society's abdomen. Art grows into the abdomen. The secret of the upper belly is its abdomen. Art is revolutionary up to the abdomen. Society has inserted into it expressionism, $a = o = expr.- = abdomen = hemorrhoidal$ suppository.

HEHEHE: Expressionist poets write because expressionist non-poets are not silent. Heaven, hell and logabouting—threefold lyrical shouting—Däublerbrilliantine is the star—lightwellwerfel is afar—Becher needs to learn rubinern, dada.

IHEHE: Waldenism autosecessionizes each pre-Waldenism while maintaining American bookkeeping. Its composition can be found on page three of the general catalogue of the Grands Magasins des Quatre Saisons for 1920 and contributions are only considered by sending in the full amount for a year's subscriptions in stamps.

KEHEHE: Soon he   plocks   Dada
Aniunde—   in   tomatopelvis
Waldas   Toria   by   mistough   ge-trickle
Koloman   Psilander   Hodenberg   Rockdada

LEHEHE: Humanitarians! Ce qu'on dom is Dostoyevsky. The right side of the piper-demon is still 0.879 dada away from the Gulf of Biscaya (across Europe). The International Dada Association resolved at its last meeting to paint a toilet seat on the Biscaya. Dada.

MEHEHE: There is no "activist" art. The artist is part of life which he destroys. Activism is the mark of all that is alive. The prattle about activism shows us that blasting the womb becomes the vital question for the new. The constricted activism of the womb finds our activism ready. The old covers itself and calls itself "life in any case." Only life and lives to the full (expressionism for the expressionist). Egocentric act: a gentleman . . . no lady. "Life in any case" exists as grub for the new. The old wastes away to the materiatur of its Anti-christ. Kyrie eleison Antichrist!

NEHEHE: Ideonopolis is burning. Ideonopolis never burns. Einstein is a cigar and cuts himself off. Eljen Karolyi! Down with Ideonopolis! Down with the idionome art. . . . Let us stuff Manet. Let us, let us. Painting is not worth a single hare's button. Dada=hare's button. Franz Marc is the founder of the cul de Berlin and is carried by women in front of their wombs To hinder. The behind. Read the Dada manifestos. 0.000001 dada=chemically pure. Long live the iadede! caracho! cocha bamba!!!

(Translated by Henry Marx)

Dramatic Scene

Kurt Schwitters

MAN: (*Pukes.*)
WOMAN: Clean that up!
MAN: I feel sick.
WOMAN: Clean that up!
MAN: I feel so sick.
WOMAN: Pig, hurry up!
MAN: I must vomit.
WOMAN: You soil my home.
MAN: I feel so sick.
WOMAN: And I spit at you.
MAN: And I must puke.
WOMAN: And I spew into your trap.
MAN: Hold me!
WOMAN: Laundry Lady!
MAN: You, you console me.
WOMAN: I will beat you.
MAN: Oh, you are good.
WOMAN: Pig, hog!
MAN: Oh, you!
WOMAN: Shut up, camel.
MAN: I have to puke again.
WOMAN: (*Beating him.*) How it whizzes.
MAN: Ow.
WOMAN: How it slashes.
MAN: Good wife!
WOMAN: Swine.

(Translated by Eelka Lampe)

Pastoral Play

Kurt Schwitters

THE LITTLE SHEPHERDESS: Here I tended my sheepeepeep. (*Looks around, to the right, to the left.*)

SHEPHERDESS: Here I tended my sheepeepeep. (*Takes her time looking around.*)

SHEPHERDESS:
Whaaat?
Here I tended my sheepeepeep.
My sheepeepeep
sheepeepeep.
(*Yawns.*) Oohhh, what a bore!
(*Jumps up, dances, sings.*) trallala, tiederallala trallalalala!
(*Pause.*)
Here I tended my sheepeepeep.
Isn't anyone coming?
Ah, yes.
my sheepeepeep.

(*Boy walks in.*)

BOY: Good day.
SHEPHERDESS: Good day. (*Pause.*)
BOY: At least you could make a curtsy.
SHEPHERDESS: Don't have time.
BOY: What are you up to then?
SHEPHERDESS: Here I tended my sheepeepeep.
BOY: Have fun.
SHEPHERDESS: You call it fun?
BOY: Otherwise you wouldn't do it, would you?
SHEPHERDESS: Ah, what do you know about it?
BOY: Better as you!
SHEPHERDESS: An, leave me alone.
BOY: Then make your curtsy.
SHEPHERDESS: (*Curtsies.*) Here I tended my sheepeepeep.
BOY: Be quiet.
SHEPHERDESS: (*Curtsies.*) Here I tended my sheepeepeep.
BOY: Shut up!
SHEPHERDESS: (*Curtsies.*) Here I tended my sheepeepeep.
BOY: I beat you black and blue.

SHEPHERDESS: (*Curtsies.*) Here I tended my sheepeepeep.

BOY: Maiden!

SHEPHERDESS: (*Curtsies.*) Here I tended my sheepeepeep.

BOY: (*Lifts his arm.*) Be quiet, I say!

SHEPHERDESS: (*Curtsies.*) Here I tended my sheepeepeep.

BOY: (*Beats her.*) There you go, go—go.

SHEPHERDESS: (*Blubbers, laughs.*) Because I take care of my sheep?

BOY: Quiet! (*Pause.*) And now what? (*Pause.*) Say something! (*Pause.*) Say something! (*Pause.*)

SHEPHERDESS: (*Curtsies.*) Here—I tended—my sheepeepeep.

BOY: Maiden!

SHEPHERDESS: (*Takes sheep and walks off slowly.*) Here I tended my sheepeepeep.

(Translated by Eelka Lampe)

To All the Theatres of the World I Demand the MERZ-Stage

Kurt Schwitters

I demand the total combination of all artistic forces to achieve the total work of art. I demand the equality in principle of all materials, equality between complete human beings, idiots, whistling wire-netting and thought pumps. I demand the complete seizure of all materials from the double-rail welder to the three-quarter violin. I demand the most conscientious rape of technology to the point of the complete execution of fusing fusions. I demand the abstract use of critics and the indivisibility of all their essays on the mutability of the stage setting and the inadequacy of human knowledge in general.

I demand the Bismark herring.

Set up gigantic surfaces, comprehend them to the point of conceived infinity, cloak them with color, displace them threateningly and arch to destruction their smooth modesty. Snap and turbulate finite parts and twist hole-boring parts of nothingness endlessly together. Glue smoothing surfaces one on top of the other. Wire lines into movement, real movement climbs real rope of a wire mesh. Flaming lines, crawling lines, flattening lines crossed. Let lines fight among themselves and stroke each other in generous tenderness. Let dots star in between, join hands and turn themselves into lines. Bend the lines, snap and double up corners throttling whirling round a point. In the waves of a whirling storm let a line rush by, graspable of wire. Roll up balls and let them come into contact in the whirling air. Let surfaces interpenetrate one another and become one and torn apart. Boxes piled up rectangular, straight and crooked and painted. Collapsible cylinder collapses box throttles box. Put lines to pull that draw a net and paint it blue. Nets encircle and constrict the torments of St. Anthony. Let nets billow and flow out in lines grow dense in surfaces, net the nets. Let veils waft, soft folds fall, let cotton wool drip and water sparkle. Roll air soft and white through thousand-candle arc lamps. Then take wheels and axles, make them rear up and sing (water giant over-stander). Axles dance middle-wheel balls roll tub. Cogwheels scent cogs, find a sewing machine that is yawning. Twisting itself upwards or stooped, the sewing machine beheads itself, feet uppermost. Take a dentist's drill, a mincing machine, crack-scratchers from the streetcar, omnibuses and automobiles, bicycles, tandems and their tires, including wartime utility tires, and deform them. Take lights and deform them in the most brutal manner. Drive locomotives into one another, let window and door curtains spider-webs dance with window frames and break whimpering glass. Make steam-boilers explode to produce railway smoke. Take petticoats and other similar things, shoes and artificial hair, also skates and throw them in the right place, where they belong, and always at the right time. As far as I'm concerned also take man-traps, spring-guns, infernal machines, the tin fish in which one bakes puddings (critics) and the funnel, naturally everything in an artistically deformed state. Hoses are also very much to be recommended. In short, take everything from the emperor's screw to the fine lady's hairnet, in each case of a size in conformity with the work.

Human beings may also be used.

Human beings may be tied to the wings. Human beings may also make an appearance, even in their everyday situation, may speak with two legs, even in sensible sentences.

Now begin to marry off the materials to each other. For instance, marry the oilcloth sheet to the building society, bring the lamp-cleaner into a relationship with the marriage between Anna Blume and the concert pitch A. Give the balls to the surface to eat and have a cracked corner destroyed by twenty-two candlepower arc lamps. Make people walk on their hands and wear hats on their feet, like Anna Blume. (Cataracts.) Foam is sprayed.

And now begins the glow of musical saturation. Organs behind the stage sing and say: "Phutt, phutt." The sewing machine rattles on in front. A man in one wing says "Bah." Another suddenly appears and says: "I'm stupid." (Copyright reserved.) A priest kneels between them the wrong way round and cries and prays loudly: "O mercy seething distonishment hallelujah lad, lad weds drops of water." A water-pipe uninhibitedly drips monotonously. Eight. Drums and flutes flash death, and a streetcar driver's pipe shines brightly. A jet of ice-cold water runs down the back of the man in one wing into a pot. He sings C sharp, D, D sharp, E flat, the whole worker's song. Under the pot a gas flame has been lit to boil the water, and a melody of violins shimmers pure and as delicate as a girl. A veil spreads latitudes. The glow in the center boils a deep dark red. There is a soft rustling. The long sighs of violins swell and die away. Light darkens stage, the sewing machine is also dark.

I demand unity in the forming of space.

I demand unity in the molding of time.

I demand unity in the mating question in respect of deformation, copulation, overlapping.

This is the Merz stage such as our time needs. I demand revision of all the theatres in the world on the basis of the Merz idea.

I demand immediate abolition of all bad conditions.

Above all, however, I demand the immediate establishment of an international experimental stage for the working out of the Merz total work of art. I demand the establishment of Merz theatres in every sizable town for the unimpeachable performance of every kind of exhibition. (Children Half-Price.)

(Translated by Michael Bullock)

Kurt Schwitters

DADA IN PARIS
1920-24

Francis Picabia design for *Relâche*

Dada in Paris, 1920-24

It was in Paris that Dada developed into a movement with a real dramatic literature. In some ways, their texts incorporated the techniques that the Dadas of Zurich and Germany had used to destroy theatrical illusion. Georges Ribemont-Dessaignes's *The Mute Canary* was written nearly a year before the Paris Dadas began their manifestations in 1920 but it remained the purest example of the movement's dramatic work in France. It was first staged by the Dadas at the twenty-fifth anniversary of *Ubu Roi* on March 27, 1920 at the Théâtre de l'Oeuvre. Also on that program was André Breton and Philippe Soupault's *If You Please*, which appeared in two separate translated pieces.

Although French critics have declared Roger Vitrac's *Free Entry* a Surrealist play because of its dream sequences, in fact the author has denied its Surrealist associations. For one, it was written in 1922, more than a year before Surrealism proclaimed itself. So it seems to fall into the chasm of Dada and Surrealist movements, and has features of both. Moreover, its production history is not clear. Tristan Tzara's *Handkerchief of Clouds*, his final Dada text, was staged at the Théâtre de la Cigale in 1924. The performance was largely ignored since Dada's potential for provocation had waned in the years 1921 to 1924.

The last Dada-like activity in Paris, Francis Picabia's *Relâche*, was presented by the Swedish Ballet on December 4, 1920. Staged like a grandiose ballet with film intervals shot by René Clair, *Relâche* itself had no formal text. This section includes the *Relâche* scenario and Picabia's instructions to Clair on the nature of the film.

The Mute Canary

Georges Ribemont-Dessaignes

(A double ladder is in the middle of the stage.)

RIQUET: Ah! Life is as dull as an old tooth.

BARATE: A gold tooth.

RIQUET: No, an old tooth.

BARATE: But gold doesn't glitter, Riquet.

RIQUET: Barate, life is as dull as a toenail.

BARATE: My toenails are rosy and glittering.

I am ignored. Men have no instinct.

RIQUET: Tsch, tsch, you are beautiful, Barate, my little Baratie. You look a little like a bat searching for a cantharis.

Kr, kr, Barate, kr.

And your eyes are soft like the hair of an ape.

BARATE: This is how men talk of love.

I don't like love. I am a harp.

RIQUET: Kékéké, Barate, Kr.

BARATE: Leave me alone. What time is it?

RIQUET: I am going hunting.

BARATE: I am asking you what time is it? Forget your hunting, poor nut!

RIQUET: It's the time when the lions go to drink.

Hussy!

BARATE: Aren't you ashamed to play games by hunting lions and then coming home with forest stinkbugs or lady bugs. What time is it?

RIQUET: Trash! Trash! It's your time. Go show your calves to your shadow to entice it. This is the moment when desire goes down to your womb and goes to your head.

Me, I'm not crazy. I'm going hunting.

BARATE: Braggart!

RIQUET: Ah, you are insulting me? I will kill you! Whore!

BARATE: I will tear out your eyes. I will cut off your . . . *(They hit each other with their fists, grab each other's hair, then, seized with fear, they fall on their knees, one in front of the other.)*

RIQUET: Mercy, Barate, pardon me. You aren't what I said!

BARATE: I know it very well. I am Messalina! But, Riquet, don't kill me. I was teasing you. I know that you're the killer of panthers.

RIQUET: Yes.

BARATE: Go hunting. But do you know what time it is?

RIQUET: Yes, yes. It is exactly the right time. One no longer distinguishes one lover from another. Go.

My damascened musket from Morocco, and a Shantung silk snare! Poet!

Oh, over there, oh, oh, is that an ostrich flying in the sky?

I was forgetting! Barate. I am returning . . .

BARATE: Why aren't you going hunting?

RIQUET: I was forgetting, Madame, that I must attend a meeting of the privy council. Are we letting the Turks stay in Europe? This is the question that I'll settle.

BARATE: Riquet! . . .

RIQUET: Would you dare jest? I'm crazy, right?

Say it, go on say it!

BARATE: Ah, ah, stars are tearing my heart to pieces.

RIQUET: Nevertheless, I will take my damascened musket and silk snare for fear of losing an opportunity. And I want these gentlemen, the Delegates to the Conference, to believe as you do, Madame, that I am a skillful hunter. (*He climbs majestically toward the top of the ladder and sits on the top rung.*)

BARATE: My husband has gone out. Gone out from himself, prisoner of something else.

Men are all like that, whether astronomers or veterinarians, to a certain degree.

He will soon return, and I'll say to him:

Scratch me under my armpit.

That is a sign of hierarchy and the use of power.

And our difference.

I am free.

I like nothing. I don't like love.

To like love is to paint in black on a blackboard.

I am a realist.

I detest men because they don't all die right after making love.

Not because of sadism, but to simplify the choice.

The average duration of man on earth is very short.

Twice on the same heart and near the same chin, what nausea!

The sad thing is that as yet no man has responded to my offers of each evening. They don't understand the hardship of being important and then, nevertheless, being rejected immediately after having been used without the hope of laundering.

Men are as dumb as eunuchs.

They are roosters.

A handsome and vigorous one to whom I said: "Do you know that you are in the arms of Messalina?" answered, "Open them. You shouldn't have said it."—And he left for somewhere else.

Is it necessary, in order to please them, to put on a hat made of pheasant plumes?

Or to walk around with a nude belly painted with garlands of roses?

To show or to hide?

Ah, I am quite perplexed.

But I am Messalina. That, at least, is certain. (*She wraps herself in veils, and walks up and down. Then she sits on a lower rung of the ladder and looks in front of herself with a melancholy air.*

From above on the ladder:)

RIQUET: In truth, Gentlemen,

I am at the pinnacle of Power, and reign over your grace

Archiepiscope and Emperor.

I feel rolling back and forth in my brains

(The alternative spirits of Confucius and of Caesar.)

Thus, I can talk to you about Science, which I possess, and about Knowledge that I draw up by means of a thousand little pumps

Subtle like the tubular tongue of twilight butterflies.

You speak of Turks, and why they are decidedly contrary to moral civilization.

I'm getting to the point.

There I am.

There is a long line passing through my middle, crossing my nose, my Adam's apple, my navel, and other essential organs.

It penetrates below into the ground and above the sky.

Each point of the world has, by the intersection of its coordinates, a place marked on this stem and its exact value established.

And each point becomes truth, that is to say, abstraction

And I, by the single fact that this thermometric line goes through the organs that I have mentioned

Am conscious of all values.

That is why the Turks who refuse to recognize this system of notation eminently favorable to Progress

Will be hunted, and they will leave Europe.

BARATE: Who is this telegraphic male?

RIQUET: Right, Marshal?

BARATE: Well, I know a cafe nearby where one drinks hot wine.

RIQUET: The difficulty with this scaffolding is, you see, in moving over to see one's self from a distance.

BARATE: This is only a drunken coachman.

Drunkenness is not advantageous to love. The poetry of poets is not the kind I like.

RIQUET: But in any case, one is certain. That is, that beyond one's self, —

There is nothing.

To act, then, is a convenience.

Simply turn one eye or the other, or lean your head toward the right or toward the left

And you displace the entire sky along with yourself.

This is mechanical government. I am the archiepiscope of the entire world.

BARATE: This proclaimer seems insensible to sensual pleasure.

He thinks I am an enemy and says to himself that, if ever pleasure would fall between us, I would be so relentless at it that there wouldn't be anything left for him.

Why do males always need to sing?

It is fine when they don't take themselves seriously, otherwise a part of their usefulness goes adrift.

The Jews lie in assuring us that man was created first.

Why is the earth round?

The circle is a female. (*A Negro appears carrying a little cage. It is Ocre.*)

BARATE: Besides, here is the first man I see!

RIQUET: Mr. Delegate of Iceland, hail!

OCRE: Madame Virgin, listen to me.

BARATE: I am yours, my friend!

RIQUET: Come and take a seat, dear Senator.

BARATE: Come sit down near me, and tell me your name, beautiful black.

OCRE: I am Mr. Gounod, music composer.

RIQUET: Another nation dissatisfied with its fate and wanting independence.

BARATE: You're handsome and strong. You smell of coconut.

OCRE: Are you the Virgin or St. Cecile?

BARATE: Oh, oh, there is some mistake. I am Messalina. Tell me your name.

Tell me your nickname so I can whisper it in your ear.

OCRE: I told you that I was the composer Gounod.

BARATE: It's a pretty name. Do you come from America or from Senegal?

OCRE: I've completely forgotten where I come from. But I am Gounod, and I am going out for the evening.

BARATE: Well, Gounod, you are a handsome Negro. I'm crazy about you.

OCRE: Why do you call me a Negro? Do you want to hurt me?

Don't you believe that I am Gounod? Look, I'll sing for you . . .

BARATE: Don't sing. Love me. Come, you have dallied too long. I am Messalina. You don't know, then, what Messalina is?

OCRE: Are you sure that you aren't St. Cecile?

BARATE: Messalina is a chic woman who goes out at night to give herself up to debauchery, while her husband, tired, slumbers. It's I.

OCRE: Ah!

BARATE: I love you, Gounod. I am very passionate.

OCRE: Yes.

BARATE: I love pleasure.

OCRE: You don't know it, but you must be Marguerite. (*He sings.*)

Hail chaste and pure dwelling! (*They embrace each other.*)

RIQUET: Ah, you see, my friends. I am in love with truth, I feed only on realities.

The most necessary one is not to know the quarrels between various existing things

But to rule them for my own end.

It isn't vain that the Verb exists. It is useless, for the sake of emotions and feelings, to judge and analyze whatever is hidden under the intermediate reasons lying between the causes and the results.

It is sufficient to announce the conclusion with a great sound of trumpets.

And the listeners' foreheads will waddle in the light.

OCRE: Who is that up there?

BARATE: A priest.

OCRE: It's Mephistopheles.

RIQUET: To be free is nothing. But liberty is all!

OCRE: Don't kiss me like that, you'll overturn my cage.

BARATE: What's this?

OCRE: It's my most precious possession.

It's a cage where a canary sleeps.

BARATE: A canary?

RIQUET: You should use words and only present their meaning to your adversaries.

OCRE: It is a mute canary that was given to me.

By my whistling all my melodies to him, he's learned them by heart.

BARATE: If he's mute, how do you know that he knows them by heart, since he can't repeat them?

OCRE: It's his way. He is mute, and I know that he now knows all my music.

A mute canary is excessively rare. It's an amazing and discreet animal, a very close friend.

RIQUET: All the great intellects of humanity have acted as I told you. Socrates and Marcus Aurelius and Boussuet.

They certainly didn't like the Turks.

There's a European civilization and an Asian one.

BARATE: Do you see how this little animal is looking at us with a moist eye?

RIQUET: Here good has one importance and bad has another.

OCRE: Right now he thinks he's Juliet's nightingale.

RIQUET: Over there good and bad can have the same importance.

BARATE: His throat is quivering as if he were going to sing.

OCRE: He sings, in fact, but one doesn't hear him.

RIQUET: If you combine intelligence and instinct as they do, all is lost.
The conquered palaces collapse, and civilization vanishes.
Spirit above.
Appearances below.

BARATE: To see him puff up his throat, I believe that I myself know what he's going to warble.

OCRE: He sings with his soul and his feelings.

BARATE: It is so beautiful that I think I'm going to cry.

RIQUET: But you, all so highly placed heads, gather around me.
Sovereigns of Japan, the Cape, Uruguay, Siam, etc.
Although sovereigns and bearers of truth, you are only imposters and clowns.
One must know, though, how to use this truth.
There is only one truth and I am the one who holds it, graduated on my vertical thermometer line.
It is truth, indeed, precisely because it cannot stand other truths. This is why I consider you as nothing.
It enables me to act in one way and to prevent you from acting in the same way, and I am right.

BARATE: Art, it inclines toward love.

OCRE: Yes, it's beautiful. Give me your lips.

BARATE: And are you the one who has written all this music that he sings?

OCRE: Yes, I am Gounod.

BARATE: How beautiful! It doesn't surprise me from a man like you.

RIQUET: I am coming with my street lamp. Your frightened shadow comes to take shelter under your feet.
My truth walks with me. Yours, following your steps,
Is variable in my eyes. Your co-ordinates for each point in the world vary each second.
Can I rely on you, little microscopes,
Fabulous candle wicks, monocles for the poor!
Here I am, I am coming! I am unchanged.
I am the great Macroscope!

BARATE: I believe I hear the planets and the stars singing in the sky.

OCRE: Perhaps. I am sure that right now he's singing the cavantina from *Romeo and Juliet*.

BARATE: How delightful! . . . How I love you! . . . How I love you!

OCRE: My line of business isn't love, it's music.

BARATE: But you do like me a little bit?

RIQUET: I no longer have anything to tell them. I'm going on a hunting trip.

OCRE: I don't know if it's love.

RIQUET: I hear a snapping noise in the bushes.

OCRE: Do you know the Queen of Sheba?

BARATE: No. What is she?

OCRE: Perhaps you resemble her.

BARATE: I told you that I was Messalina. Ah! I love you.

OCRE: Is Messalina an opera? I didn't write it.

BARATE: You are getting on my nerves! I'm the Empress Messalina. And I'll possess you, no matter how unloving you are. Come, handsome Numidian. (*She leaps on him. A struggle.*)

RIQUET: There's some panther in the bushes. Yes, I see its shadow.

Oh, I'm in the middle of the jungle. I see it before me as large as life.

There are two panthers fighting. I'm going to make you a double hit.

To you, Africa! (*He fires twice.*)

OCRE: Hail, oh my last morning! (*He dies.*)

BARATE: Unfortunate Messalina! (*She dies.*)

RIQUET: *Touché!*

These aren't panthers, but some screech-owls. I recognize their cries.

This foretells misfortune. Let's get out of here. (*He gets down from the ladder.*)

And, besides, I still have something to tell them. They remain quiet after my oration. They are surprised and troubled.

I am the master of Europe. (*He stumbles against the cage.*)

Oh, what, what is that? An animal?

Oh, Oh, how marvelous! An animal that I've caught in my snare!

Heavens! I've never seen anything like it! He's frightening and he rolls his wide-open eyes.

I was rightly telling my unbelieving wife, the old Barate.

I am the great hunter.

Oh, oh, what is he saying? He's puffing up his throat. He's angry.

But he's repulsive with such eyes.

They're the eyes of a toad!

Yes, I know what he is! A hydra, I've caught a hydra in the snare.

An enormous and dreadful hydra!

At least that's worthy of a sovereign whose own goal of sovereignty

Is to stand among all, high above all

Like a great macroscope. (*He leaves carrying the cage.*)

(Translated by Victoria Nes Kirby)

If You Please

André Breton & Philippe Soupault

Act One

(*A drawing room. 5 p.m. Door at the back. Windows at right and left. Two armchairs. A cassock. A low table. A lamp. Mirrors.*)

CHARACTERS

Paul: Forty years old. Hairline moustache; stoops, has gray hair.
Valentine: Twenty-five years old.
Francois: Twenty-seven years old, clean-shaven.

SCENE ONE

PAUL: I love you. (*Long kiss.*)
VALENTINE: A cloud of milk in a cup of tea. (*Pause.*)
PAUL: How hard do you think it is for me to choose between the passage of the Tropics and those more distant dawns that dazzle me as soon as you open your eyes? The white phosphorus of other women's lips had made love impossible for me up to now. Uncertain of finding you, I listened to the shower of tresses striking the windows of my idleness and only perceived the turbulence of manufactured breezes from afar. I must confess that for a long time I have given myself over to delusive arguments between that inseparable pair, the street lamp and the gutter.
VALENTINE: Don't be afraid to speak. I know what you are going to say, but who cares! Our life rises so slowly with your eyes which look at me and forget me. You are still going to cradle me with "Remember!"—do you remember?
PAUL: You have to keep a certain distance from the wall to rouse an echo. With all those we love our hope is to be able to embrace the trunk of this supraterrestrial tree.
VALENTINE: The thousand and one nights sink into one of ours. I dreamed that we were drowning.
PAUL: It's a long time since the charming statue on top of the Tour Saint-Jacques let fall the crown of the immortals which it held in its hand . . . How do you like your new apartment?
VALENTINE: My husband's study has a view of the gardens of the Palais-Royal.

PAUL: Ah, yes! Staring at the bars again.

VALENTINE: Naughty. And those crumbs of bread for the birds: solitude? The regions of the imagination are so vast!

PAUL: (*Catching sight of one of his own grimaces in the mirror.*) It's absolutely correct to compare certain looks to lightning: they flash against the same broken branches, they make the same blonde young girls leaning against black furniture appear . . . You are more beautiful than they.

VALENTINE: I know. You like the gleaming chestnuts buried in my hair. (*Pause.*)

PAUL: Did you hear him come in?

VALENTINE: Current morality: it makes one think of a current of water.

PAUL: The charm lies in that lovely liquid song, the spelling out of the catechism by children. What do you talk about in a pinch?

VALENTINE: The patience of an angel. I have the patience of an angel. He rented a villa, a temporary one for the season. Lots of ivy. Like other men, he is the slave of his fatigue at one time and of his pleasure at another. (*Arranging a fold of her dress.*) Do you like my dress?

PAUL: (*Going to her.*) A casket of arms lined with blue velvet.

VALENTINE: Love.

PAUL: Flesh or pearls. A diver in crystal waves. Everything hangs by a thread.

VALENTINE: It's the beginning of paradise, or so it seems. The gray, slaty day has blue automobile horns; at night one flies on a silvery frond.

PAUL: What are you doing tomorrow?

VALENTINE: The department stores will be open: the youth of so many women.

PAUL: You say to the elevator starter standing near the door: "Going up, sir, if you please?"

VALENTINE: The smiles of the salespeople. Yet another coquetry. (*Pause.*) What are you thinking about?

PAUL: The sweetness of life. Everyone takes part in it. Gossamer at the height of a man's face, the song of capitals.

VALENTINE: You're like the workers who test the wheels with a hammer when the train stops.

PAUL: (*Distraught.*) I've often asked myself what might be the speed, in a fast train or in love, of the flies which fly from the rear wall to the front wall of some sleeping compartment or other. (*Coming back brusquely to her.*) You're not cold?

VALENTINE: What time is it? (*Pause.*) Paul, my happiness is as sweet as starved birds. You can play at lowering your eyes or at clenching your fists. I agree to be in despair. I've thought of you so much since the other day!

PAUL: Speak.

VALENTINE: The brilliant words I would like to say stream in the sky like the stars which you were looking at. You don't want to laugh? When you are away from me it is your laugh I hear first of all.

SCENE TWO

FRANCOIS: (*Enters with hands extended.*) My dear friends, I've come to say goodbye. (*To his wife.*) It's a pity that you're not tempted by a little promenade to Geneva. I can't resign myself to going alone.

VALENTINE: I'm so exhausted, my friend.

FRANCOIS: Even more exhausted now?

VALENTINE: Yes. I feel dizzy. My head feels like a cash register. I feel lost around here. Before Paul came a ray of sun falling on a green plant kept me going like an exciting novel.

FRANCOIS: You should take a cup of linden tea with a dash of brandy. Sometimes I feel the same way myself, and I always make myself a nice hot cup of linden tea and add several shots of brandy. It does wonders. Wouldn't you like to try it?

VALENTINE: No, thanks. I'll be all right. I feel better already. I wish you wouldn't bother about me—it makes me feel so silly.

PAUL: There's nothing silly about it. Would you like me to ring?

VALENTINE: Please don't bother.

PAUL: Really?

VALENTINE: Really.

FRANCOIS: All the same, a little cup of linden tea with a little brandy wouldn't do you any harm. (*Pause.*)

VALENTINE: What time does your train leave?

FRANCOIS: Seven thirty-three p.m.

VALENTINE: Where will you be staying?

FRANCOIS: Hotel Bristol, Geneva. I hope you won't be too bored. (*To Paul.*) See that you entertain her. (*Taking him by the arm.*) I rely on you, old chap.

VALENTINE: What are you going to do there?

FRANCOIS: Do you remember John the Coalminer? I've owed him a visit for a long time. He used to be my best friend.

VALENTINE: You've often told me about him.

FRANCOIS: :You're the one who urged me to go, and now I almost regret it. It's so easy for me not to think of anything but us. If only you'd agree to leave Paris with me! Is it really so hard to give up these activities, these parties? I'd love to see the color come back to your face and not see these dark circles under your eyes.

VALENTINE: Listening to you one would think I was in critical condition.

PAUL: It will go away. It's nerves. (*Pause.*)

FRANCOIS: (*Gets up, takes several steps, then stops in front of Valentine.*) This time tomorrow I'll be far away from you. It will be a solitude both pleasant and warm. I will feel as if I had been away from you for weeks, months, years. People will speak and be excited. The caress of the water on the bank moves and excites me already! From the terrace of my hotel I see white sails pass by on the lake. That landscape intoxicates me at sunset. After having been the great, silent lake all day, at twilight it becomes an enchanted and supernatural country. (*A knock on the door.*)

VALENTINE: Come in. (*Enter a Servant.*)

SERVANT: The carriage waits, sir. (*Francois looks at his watch.*)

VALENTINE: You must not be late.

FRANCOIS: Oh, I've got time. (*The Servant leaves. Francois, changing his tone.*) What if I telegraphed to John not to expect me? (*Pause. He appears to hesitate.*)

PAUL: Stay.

FRANCOIS: One constantly retraces one's steps, which is understandable enough. I know that for me reality is here in your friendship, and uncertitude is out there among the chattering voices and the busy faces. (*Valentine goes to the window and remains there until the beginning of the following scene, her forehead pressed against the glass.*) The railroad stations are great temptations which one resists as much as possible. On what can you rest your eyes when they've ceased to exist? One doesn't carry away any remembrance, not even a scrap of wallpaper. Nothing but the dryness of the timetable and the ability to start a conversation with any stranger. (*Sighs.*) Ah! (*Calling out.*) Valentine!

VALENTINE: What?

FRANCOIS: (*Arms extended.*) I'm going.

VALENTINE: Till Thursday. (*She gives him her forehead to kiss.*)

FRANCOIS: (*To Paul.*) So long, old chap. (*Shakes hands.*)

SCENE THREE

(*Pause. Valentine is still at the window. The door closes.*)

PAUL: Valentine!

VALENTINE: What?

PAUL: A door closes and our life begins.

VALENTINE: (*Going to him.*) I know that voice false as the clouds. (*Noise of automobile going away.*)

PAUL: Then you have not understood that all these gestures, all these words which come to you die, if you don't gather them.

VALENTINE: Look at me and I will believe in the sadness of each yes, in a-wakenings painful as sand.

PAUL: I have the right to lie to you.

VALENTINE: I have seen my image in each reflection and I am afraid not to believe you. You lie? And I want you to tell me no.

PAUL: What for? You know very well that you must suffer. One day, one hour, like a tree isolated in the country of your childhood, is worth all the distant months which are nothing but tomorrow. Doubt leans gently against you, and you will run away from it like an ingrate.

VALENTINE: I am going to find air and cold again, and I will finally know that you are no longer there.

PAUL: I am only sincere when I can lie to you. The words you love I know by heart.

VALENTINE: Speak, I beg you. Each moment of silence eats up my minutes. My heart beats as at the arrival of trains. I follow the roadbed of my dreams. The end is very near. We will not delay our partings, and sleep stretches around us.

PAUL: Listen . . .

VALENTINE: You're smiling . . .

PAUL: I cannot flee from my smile. It imposes itself on me like a dream.

VALENTINE: Do we know why I suffer? I don't even know why I tremble. I'm frightened. Do you hear?

PAUL: (*Dryly.*) Yes, perfectly.

VALENTINE: I wanted to tell you . . .

PAUL: (*Same tone.*) What?

VALENTINE: You know. Will you be able to come see us often?

PAUL: (*Same tone.*) I don't know. We'll see.

VALENTINE: I'd like to leave you right away and not hear your words, which fall heavily on my ears. The sound of your steps hurts me.

PAUL: You are so far away!

VALENTINE: I am as near to you as the ground.

PAUL: It's necessary to depart and not look back. It's a question of something else entirely. We are not concerned with tenderness: it's that vague fog which is not enough to hide the blood in our veins and the suffering of our hands.

VALENTINE: My head sinks; my eyes close. I'd like to be the horizon which you'll never reach. I would feel your painful desire and your looks.

PAUL: It's getting dark. You still seem to be speaking of the pretty moon beams of our youth. The sky is beautiful, you say (*looking out of the side of the window*), but it's really just a sunset.

VALENTINE: At least right now tears can touch you.

PAUL: One glimpses adventure and destinies in the distance. And yet it's too near. The months, the color of eyes, and the reflections of rainy days beguile us. Sometimes, in the evening, I turn out my pockets.

VALENTINE: Do you really know how late it is?

PAUL: Since you only forget our silence and the moistness of our eyelids, night can come without my caring. Mystery leaves me as cold as the branches they'll throw on our graves the next day, and the vigil candle, the rain, and the bad weather. What does all that and everything else mean? These noises behind me—do you think I fear them? I prefer to read in your face the imaginary joys and sadnesses that I have known so well. My age doesn't interest me. (*He lights a cigarette.*)

VALENTINE: I still hear you. The skeleton that you are rattling and these words that make me clench my teeth—I love them like the final moments of the night. Even at the great distance between us your encircling arms suffocate me. Is the sequel worth living? The great fire which illuminates us and sings in our flesh leaves us a husk of helpless shadows. I'm not afraid of love. Perhaps only desire exists and I am the strongest in the final analysis. Look how I am protected! At this moment you can do nothing against any single one of my actions. (*She puts her hands behind her head and turns slightly to the right, her eyes closed. A mass of hair is seen falling on the night.*) What are you going to do with me? (*Paul puts out his cigarette in an ash tray. Sound of an automobile stopping in front of the hotel. Paul slowly draws a revolver from his pocket, barely taking aim. Valentine falls without a sound. Several sharp rings are heard. Very calmly Paul puts the revolver away and relights his extinguished cigarette.*)

Act Two

(*An office at four o'clock in the afternoon. A huge map of France on the rear wall. Window at rear. Doors at right and left. Typewriter on table in front of window. A suitcase near the door. Telephone and large notebook on the desk. Armchairs, chairs.*)

Letoile: Forty years old, clean-shaven, rosette of the Legion of Honor, horn-rimmed glasses.

A Typist: dark, pretty.

Lefebvre

A Man

A Lady

Two Ladies of Charity

A Young Man

Three Men

Two Policemen

A Police Inspector

An Office Boy

SCENE ONE

LETOILE: (*Dictating.*) I would be very much obliged if you would send me a favorable answer to this in the shortest possible time. Yours sincerely, etc. (*The typist goes back to her desk and starts to type.*)

SCENE TWO

LEFEBVRE: (*Having knocked several times without getting an answer, he opens the door and sticks his head in.*) O.k. if I come in, Chief? (*He comes in.*) I haven't wasted my day, Chief. Got something here which I think'll interest you. This afternoon in the country I saw some people amusing themselves by starting up two sidetracked locomotives.
LETOILE: Very good.
LEFEBVRE: It wasn't as amusing a caper as those jokers had thought, since the locomotives overturned in a ditch. If they hadn't capsized they'd have run through two houses, which would have been the crowning joy for those jokers. (*Sanctimoniously.*) It is high time that people understood that all individual wealth and force contribute to the wealth and strength of everyone, and that people are simply depriving themselves when they drive locomotives into the streets or break the windows of the carriages when the train is late.
LETOILE: Idiot. Go and sit down in the waiting room next to the woman near the window. Get hold of her handbag and bring me the letters you'll find there. Thank you. (*Lefebvre goes out.*)

SCENE THREE

LETOILE: (*Makes a telephone call.*) Elysees 40-52. (*Pause.*) Hello! Is this the Bellegue Press? Letoile here. Take this down. I want the proofs delivered to me tomorrow at six. In the good old days, when an inhabitant of one of our little villages departed this life, the sacristan had the church bells rung. In order to let the other villagers know the age of the deceased, the number of times the death bell was tolled indicated the age of the departed, and the people said, "How old he was!" Nowadays, if the sacristans of our big city parishes followed this old custom, we would hear all too often very short death tolls and we would frequently say, "Alas! How young he was!" Nowadays one dies young. The fault lies in the conditions of our existence, which have changed. We overwork; we exhaust our strength by leading too busy a life. Let us therefore listen to the sound of other bells, joyous and comforting bells, those which we will call the happy carillons of idleness, that is to say, of the uselessness of effort. Send it to Letoile, 47 rue du Sentier. (*This whole speech must be* delivered in a crisp tone of voice. Letoile hangs up. He puts an overcoat on, turns the collar up and puts his hat on the desk; then he rings. A distinguished-looking man in his forties enters immediately.)

SCENE FOUR

LETOILE: (*Speaks heatedly; during the whole scene his eyes do not leave the other man.*) Sir, I'm sorry to say I can't give you more than a few moments. I was about to go out when your card was sent in. Be so good as to take a seat. (*He remains standing.*)

THE MAN: Yesterday evening my wife and I came home after having been to the theatre. I should tell you that the dressing room is quite some distance from our bedroom. Before undressing, my wife put her necklace and rings on the mantelpiece. I remained in the study.

LETOILE: Excuse me, were you smoking?

THE MAN: (*After taking time to reflect.*) Yes. Several minutes later . . .

LETOILE: Several minutes, you say.

THE MAN: (*Troubled.*) Well, about ten minutes. The jewels had disappeared. (*Pause.*)

LETOILE: I would be interested in knowing to what I owe the honor of this visit.

THE MAN: (*Worried.*) You *are* Monsieur Letoile?

LETOILE: Absolutely.

THE MAN: I've come on the strength of your posters which paper all the walls, whether broken-down or not. In time of need these promises are sweeter than knowing how to swim. Everyone knows that Letoile is in possession of the same powers as God: he sees all, hears all—and no one suspects it. For a long time now I've considered you the hero of our modern romance of knight errantry. You will pull me out of this mess in the twinkling of an eye.

LETOILE: Matters such as this concern the police. At any other time, my dear sir, it will be a pleasure to be of service to you. (*He goes to open the door. The man rises, bows, and leaves.*)

SCENE FIVE

(*Letoile takes off his overcoat. Lefebvre enters, gives him some letters, and goes out without a word. Letoile puts the letters in a drawer.*)

SCENE SIX

(*A knock on the door. Enter the office boy.*)

THE OFFICE BOY: There's two ladies who want to speak to you about a charity.

LETOILE: (*Rubbing his hands.*) Show them in at once. (*The two ladies enter. They are old and shabby and carry little notebooks in their hands. Without a word Letoile shows them to a seat. He goes back to his armchair, lights a cigar, and waits. The first lady coughs. In a cutting tone, blowing huge puffs of smoke.*) The smoke doesn't bother you? (*The lady appears very bothered.*)

SECOND LADY:
Have you sometime, sir, when evening falls,
Observed the hungry creep along the walls?
You see them pass and pass again outside the park.
Haggard, tattered, shielding with alarm
A little infant child to keep it from all harm:
A burden dear, with rags wrapped up all in vain,
Which yet sleeps peacefully in snow and rain,
Finding, next to the breast so withered by her grief,
His only warmth, his one protective reef!
She holds her hand out to you. Suppliant and mute
Under the pale gas lamps which light her route,
She glides along with speed and in the shadowy halls
Of ruined houses, or along the walls
She flits, her face expressive of her grief . . .

LETOILE: How much do you want?

FIRST LADY: My God, your heart must dictate the amount, sir. (*Letoile opens a drawer and offers them a banknote without saying a word. The two ladies thank him profusely, put away the money, and prepare to go.*)

LETOILE: One moment. (*He rings. Enter the office boy.*) Get two policemen instantly. (*To the ladies.*) You'll explain yourselves at the station house.

THE TWO LADIES: (*Nonplussed.*) But sir, what do you take us for?

LETOILE: Yes or no, are you or are you not thieves?

FIRST LADY: (*Taking a card from her bag.*) We are licensed by the Municipal Authorities.

LETOILE: (*Having carefully examined the card.*) In that case, you'll give the 500 francs back. (*The ladies tremblingly return the money. Letoile crumples it up while he keeps looking at them and then throws it into the fire. The ladies, discountenanced, sit down. A pause. Letoile opens a newspaper. The ladies leave, one behind the other. The first one drops her notebook and the second picks it up.*)

SCENE SEVEN

(*Enter a lady wearing a small veil.*)

THE LADY: I would like to speak to you in confidence.

LETOILE: Very good, Madame. (*Turning to the Typist.*) You will take down our conversation. (*Peremptorily.*) I am listening, Madame.

THE LADY: (*Holding a handkerchief.*) I've been married scarcely a year and I now understand that my husband feels an honest and upright love for another woman. Doubtless he doesn't know it yet himself, but I can measure the depths of the enormous abyss that already lies between us better than anyone. There is nothing for me to do but sacrifice myself. (*A pause; some tears.*) That's why, simply, I've come to see you. I must leave my husband. I will grant him independence.

LETOILE: You are absolutely determined to get a divorce?

THE LADY: Absolutely.

LETOILE: Doubtless you believe that you will be making your husband happy. What a misapprehension! It is wrong to suppose that the more independent a man is, the happier he is. Happiness consists in balance; it involves habits, a routine—in brief, a curb on the need for pleasure. If a couple does not feel itself bound by an authority stronger than their own caprice, then the ease with which they can separate renders the least irritation intolerable to them. Liberty is beautiful as the sun, but it does not behoove you to draw your husband away from his habits. Everything in its place is a bond that is sweeter than woman's breath. Everything that exists today—the fold of a curtain, the light in its accustomed corner—is then once and for all dead to him. All that is left to him is a memory which pursues him like a ghostly bat. . . . You may count on me, Madame: in approximately two months the divorce will be decreed in your favor. I will call you in for the indispensable formalities.

THE LADY: (*Who has been giving signs of doubt.*) Listen, I'm going to think it over again. I'll see.

LETOILE: (*Dryly.*) I wouldn't advise it. Reflect—that's just always retracing your steps.

THE LADY: I don't know what to do anymore. (*Tears.*)

LETOILE: (*Energetically.*) You have nothing to do. Just sign a few pieces of paper. (*He rises. The Lady rises in her turn, undecided. She leaves.*)

SCENE EIGHT

LETOILE: Take this down. (*He dictates.*) Publicity Office, forty rue de Richard Lenoir. One hundred thousand francs REWARD. A mysterious theft has occurred during the last few days in the home of the Chardin-Lamothe family, one hundred seventy-two boulevard Pereire, Paris. A casket disappeared under the most mysterious circumstances. Paragraph. Two young women going under the assumed names of Marcelle de Livry and Blanche Valfort, also known as Bigmouth, are suspected of having committed the crime. Paragraph. Since audacity is more than ever to be encouraged, one must predict a brilliant career for them. Anyone instrumental in uncovering their traces may put in his claim for the promised reward by communicating with Monsieur Letoile, forty-seven rue du Sentier. Period. (*The bell rings.*)

SCENE NINE

(*The office boy enters and puts a vase of flowers on the desk. Letoile puts a flower in his buttonhole. Enter a smiling Young Man with a well-groomed blond mustache.*)

LETOILE: (*After having shaken hands.*) I think I may have what you are looking for. Delighted to be of service in any little thing. I find your company really agreeable.

THE YOUNG MAN: What color are her eyes. (*He remains standing; Letoile leans easily against the desk.*)

LETOILE: Ah! People keep saying that society is going to the dogs, but it's organisms like yourself that reassure me of its health. In you, as in the woman I've destined for you, I distinguish the elements of a force which will find full scope for action in your marriage. Young man, you show signs of deep wisdom: life is a path full of twists and turns—the views are varied and the traveler loves to communicate his impressions. If the path is dull, it seems not so long when trodden with a companion. If several paths are seen, you consult together, and if some difficulty comes up you encourage each other and thus surmount the obstacle more easily. Singing together, the two companions climb up the first slope of the hill; when they reach old age, leaning on each other's arms, with halting steps they descend the opposite slope, chatting together of their memories of other times, their faces lighted up with an eternal smile.

THE YOUNG MAN: Is she musical?

LETOILE: In a very few days we will have the meeting in a public place—a teahouse, a park, a theatre. The presentation by Letoile. Smiles . . . compliments . . . what a happy coincidence! How often each one has heard the other spoken of! Charming!

THE YOUNG MAN: (*Moved.*) How can I ever thank you, Monsieur Letoile?

LETOILE: (*Shaking his hand.*) You owe me nothing, my friend; it's a pleasure for me.

SCENE TEN

(*A knock on the door.*)

LETOILE: Come in. (*Enter the Office Boy.*)

THE OFFICE BOY: The police are here, sir.

LETOILE: Good; have them come in. (*To the Policemen.*) Arrest that man.

THE YOUNG MAN: What's going on? You're out of your mind.

LETOILE: Resistance is useless. (*To the Policemen.*) I make a formal accusation against this man for murdering his mistress, Madame Valentine Saint-Cervan. My deposition will be brief. I will rejoin you at the station house in a moment. (*Calling them back.*) Take this suitcase with you. It contains the evidence for conviction.

SCENE ELEVEN

(*Letoile walks up and down for a moment and then stops in front of the map of France.*)

TYPIST: May I have the afternoon off tomorrow, sir?

LETOILE: I'll allow you to go to the Bois de Boulogne.

TYPIST: Thank you, sir.

LETOILE: (*Looking fixedly at her.*) You are beautiful, my child. (*She lowers her eyes.*) Are you afraid of me? (*She comes nearer.*) Do you understand what goes on here? Fanaticism is a magic lantern in the light of which boredom takes on disquieting shapes like this map of France. You think of nothing but casual friends with whom one stretches out on the grass or makes jokes with. I see no other inconveniencing factor in that than the clouds of dust raised by the cars on the road.

TYPIST: We've had a wonderful time today.

LETOILE: It happens from time to time that I pace up and down in front of houses or among the trees on the square. The strollers smiled at my impatience, but I wasn't waiting for anyone.

TYPIST: I'll never forget you.

LETOILE: Like the wind, forgetfulness blows the leaves of bills over the doorsteps of credit, then chases them all away.

TYPIST: There are other whirlwinds—the intoxication of parties and the contradictory orders that you give. It's like when one is lying in the arms of pleasure close to midnight, when the concern of mother and brothers doesn't count any more; one loses all sense of wrongdoing and leans back with closed eyes against a comfort of a tree. The department stores could catch fire; all the prayers could be prayed: the earthly paradise is far. For the time being one returns to the brightly lit bars and in one's heart broods about the barbarous acts which are being committed all over the world.

LETOILE: Your way of unfolding the newspaper enchants me, but this young man whom I've had arrested hasn't done anything to you.

TYPIST: Chance dictates the colors that we like. It does not depend on us to stake our happiness on the green. (*She goes and cowers in a corner of the stage.*)

LETOILE: The appearance of danger is like your black hair and these little hands along the wall. (*She extends her arms along the wall.*) What's that supposed to mean: No Thoroughfare? Your adorable silences would tarnish the crown of martyrdom as easily as a little pocket mirror. But there is no exultation on my part. Action means as little to me as anything else, and if you will look carefully at my tie you will not believe that you see the pretty cashmere of lost illusions.

SCENE TWELVE

LEFEBVRE: (*Enters without knocking.*) Me and the boys would like to have a a word with you, Chief. (*Courtois, Hirsch, and Levy follow him in.*) You've made us promise to follow your orders without arguing, but one can't always work without knowing what one's doing.

LETOILE: What do you want me to tell you?

HIRSCH: It's like in a prison around here. Moving a pile of rocks around by the sweat of your brow—if you're not condemned right away to do the opposite. As soon as you get on to one track, you're told to get off it.

LETOILE: What do you care? Aren't you getting paid?

COURTOIS: All the same, you don't feel right at having all that useless money pass through your hands, as if you were a bank teller. It's hard to give back the pocketbooks. When these acts of apparent honesty are carefully considered, who knows if they won't get the better of us? (*Murmurs of approbation.*) The other day you had us each disguise ourselves and follow each other around. (*Agitation.*)

LETOILE: (*Getting up and, with his hands in his pockets, looking out the window.*) I don't owe anyone an explanation. If you're not satisfied you can leave. (*He sits down again. A pause.*) Lefebvre, be at the Buttes-Chaumont at nightfall. See that you make yourself agreeable to the first person you see loitering on the bridge. Find means to bring him here. Understood?

LEFEBVRE: (*Questions his companions with his eyes.*) Yes, Chief.

LETOILE: (*To Levy.*) A spherical drop of water takes two minutes to drop from the cloud where it is formed. Assuming that before falling this drop splits into ten separate drops of equal size, how long would it take this bunch of droplets to fall? I need to know the answer to this problem before tonight. (*To the other two.*) Thank you very much. (*They leave.*)

SCENE THIRTEEN

(*The telephone rings.*)

LETOILE: (*Into the telephone.*) Hello! Yes, it's me. . . . Not bad, thanks . . . Nothing . . . Later? Who knows . . . I've seen all the trees lose their leaves for a long time. . . . Over there that's all that one dreams, but over there doesn't exist. There will never be anything but here . . . I observe the drops of rain which are all the moments of my life run down the windowpanes. . . . The hours which will never return anymore seem like centuries. . . . So much the better! I no longer want the pleasures I've desired for such a long time because they are within my reach. I know tomorrow, the day after tomorrow, and all the other days. . . . The future is this same mirror that is always before one's eyes. . . . My ears buzz with the sound of the bells of pride. . . .

SCENE FOURTEEN

LEFEBVRE: (*Rushing in.*) The cops, Chief—you've just time to get out of here.
LETOILE: (*In a faraway tone.*) You're sure of what you're saying? (*A knock at the door.*) Who's there? (*Silence.*) Come in.
THE INSPECTOR: Monsieur Letoile?
LETOILE: That's me, in person.
THE INSPECTOR: I have a warrant for your arrest. You will please come with me.
LETOILE: Just the time to give one order and then I'm ready.
THE INSPECTOR: You are accused . . .
LETOILE: What does that matter to me?

Act Three

(*A cafe at three o'clock in the afternoon. Doors at rear and at left. Clock at right. Two card players under the clock.*)

Maxime: Thirty years old, blond, Van Dyke beard.
Gilda: A whore.
An Algerian Peddler

(*When the curtain rises the card players are playing in silence. Gilda, who is sitting at another table, is drinking a red liqueur. It is raining.*)

SCENE ONE

(*The Waiter passes through and wipes one of the tables. He lifts the curtain and looks out.*)

FIRST PLAYER: Waiter, a beer. (*The game starts again. The Waiter brings the drink, sits down at the back, and opens a newspaper. Silence.*)

SECOND PLAYER: If I'd known that, I wouldn't have trumped.

FIRST PLAYER: You made a mistake. (*He shuffles. A newsboy is heard shouting "La Patrie." Gilda takes a small mirror from her bag and puts on powder and lipstick.*)

SCENE TWO

(*Enter Maxime, an umbrella in his hand. He sits down in the back.*)

MAXIME: Let's see . . . give me a vermouth and something to write with. (*He seems to be groping for his words and keeps looking around. His observation of Gilda becomes more and more marked.*) It's too dark back there. (*He sits down nearer Gilda.*) What weather!

GILDA: It's raining. (*A pause.*)

MAXIME: Aren't you bored?

GILDA: Why?

MAXIME: Are you waiting for someone?

GILDA: No. (*She smiles.*)

MAXIME: (*Sitting down opposite her.*) With your permission. (*A pause.*)

GILDA: I was dreaming that I was still in boarding school. I was wearing that lace collar one last time. They kept a sharp eye on my correspondence: an unknown man will climb over the garden wall this evening. He said to me: "You've been crying because of my mother-of-pearl cheeks." Night will fall. Soon there will be nothing but the windmills.

MAXIME: You can take it or leave it. Interior elegance and the maddest acts of despair. To leave the church throwing candy around.

GILDA: You're not like the others.

MAXIME: How can one not say to oneself several times every day: that won't come back again! (*A pause.*)

GILDA: You haven't finished your letter.

MAXIME: What's the good of giving a sign of life for too long a time? It's 3:15 and I see you.

GILDA: The instinct to please is like a pit. Believe me, rings are nothing. In Paris, on the big boulevards, there is a slope so gentle that almost no one can stop himself from sliding down it.

MAXIME: The most touching maps of the world are the silver globes in which the waiter arranges a napkin from time to time. Caged birds love these little gleaming spheres. It comes to the same thing whether one sings with the street or the sewing machine.

GILDA: I recognize liberty by certain finer signs.

MAXIME: The kingdom of the skies is peopled with assassins. Higher up there's a swing which waits for you. Don't lift your head again.

GILDA: The photographer said: Let's not move.

MAXIME: I don't want to die.

GILDA: Someone has dared to sadden you?

MAXIME: I don't think so; I've only just come in.

GILDA: Are your eyes really that color?

MAXIME: Elbow on the table like naughty children. The fruit of a Christian primary education, if books don't lie, is everything that is golden.

GILDA: In the huts of fishermen one finds those artificial bouquets made up of periwinkles and even a bunch of grapes.

MAXIME: The globe must be lifted up if it is not transparent enough. The fountain of the Observatory at sunrise.

GILDA: The songs of the streets and of the woods are beautiful. (*A pause.*)

MAXIME: I won't love you always.

GILDA: I don't ask for any other truth when I go out than the rainbow. Somebody once told me—it was such a long time ago—that I was beautiful; today I know that I am only pretty.

MAXIME: Observe the flight of birds or the wanings of the moon.

GILDA: The numbers that one throws into one's life, the dates of days of sadness are far from my lips.

MAXIME: Corridors and clouds are my whole life. I only know the glimmer of my lamp. You are near me.

GILDA: I am big tonight and only my head exists.

MAXIME: You are a child or the drowsiness of summer.

GILDA: When you say goodbye to me in a few minutes, I will follow you until death.

MAXIME: Past and future are only the present. The market pitchmen, thirst, and all these little quotidian insects. It is day and I am there.

GILDA: Words burn me like spotlights.

MAXIME: You're still thinking about dawns. You say: Over there. I am near you.

GILDA: I dream of forests.

MAXIME: The paths in the fields of dawn. Mad animals and blind beggars listening to us.

GILDA: Why do you laugh?

MAXIME: Midday: the hour of doves and, much later, the evening. Your look and your shoulders before me. The flowers which we both love. Heat dances at full speed. Again these same thoughts which fall and fly: the butterflies of suffering and a dream sweeter than agony. (*A pause.*)

GILDA: Automobiles are silent. It will rain blood.

MAXIME: The rats chew up the vines without thinking of tomorrow. The peasant girls don't know fans. Give me your hand and I will love your life.

GILDA: Call me Gilda.
MAXIME: Listen, listen.
GILDA: I am there.
MAXIME: It's tomorrow.
GILDA: The distance, the network of cardinal points. Flags and immense expanses of bunting cover the earth. Fold your hands and breathe softly. (*A pause. For some moments Maxime has been holding the stem of an empty glass between the index and middle fingers of his right hand and has been tracing eight diagonal lines on the marble with it. A Peddler of carpets, shawls, belts, and so on, has entered. He has started to make his pitch to the Card Players.*)

SCENE THREE

(*The Algerian goes to Maxime. He shows a tiger skin which he carries on his shoulders and under which he alternately stretches out and lets fall his arm. A pause.*)

ALGERIAN: Purse. (*A pause. Maxime remains motionless.*) Rug. (*A Pause.*) Suspenders. (*He shows the suspenders. A pause. The waiter enters and sees the Algerian.*)
WAITER: Let's go—get out of here. (*The Algerian leaves slowly.*)

SCENE FOUR

MAXIME: Where do you live?
GILDA: No, no, don't.
MAXIME: What's the matter?
GILDA: (*Giving him her hand.*) Let me leave alone.
MAXIME: Waiter.
WAITER: That'll be three francs, sir. (*They get up.*)
GILDA: Don't insist, sweetheart. You'll regret it. I've got the syph.
MAXIME: Who cares? (*They leave.*)

(*A long intermission.*)

Act Four

SCENE ONE

(*The auditorium is plunged into half-darkness. The curtain rises on a front door. Two insignificant characters, one with a cane in his hand, stop in front of the door.*)

X: (*Consulting his watch.*) Look at the time, I'm leaving. (*They shake hands.*)

Y: (Paces back and forth in front of the door without saying a word. He looks upwards, rubs his arms with his hands, blows his nose.)

SCENE TWO

SPECTATOR IN THE ORCHESTRA: "That's all?" (*The pacer on stage stops, looks at the interrupter with surprise, then lifts his eyes skyward and continues pacing.*)

THE SPECTATOR: Will you be finished soon? (*One hears:* "Shhhh!")

SECOND SPECTATOR: I don't understand anything. It's idiotic. (*Someone shouts from the balcony:* "Will you please shut up!")

SECOND SPECTATOR: (*Standing.*) I do have the right to say what I think.

FROM THE BALCONY: You have the right to leave. (*The actor is stopped.*)

SECOND SPECTATOR: I paid for my seat just like you.

WIFE OF SECOND SPECTATOR: Please, Edward, be quiet.

VOICE FROM AUDIENCE: If at least it were amusing.

SECOND SPECTATOR: I repeat that I understand nothing. (*Applause.*) It is probable that I'm not the only one. (*Standing on seat.*) For some time now, under pretext of originality and independence, our fine art has been sabotaged by a bunch of individuals, whose number increases every day and who are for the most part, strange types, lazy fellows or practical jokers. (*The curtain falls. Applause.*) It is easier to get yourself talked about in this fashion than to attain true glory at the cost of hard work. Are we going to put up with the most contradictory ideas and aesthetic theories, the beautiful and the ugly, talent and force without style being placed on the same footing? I appeal to our tradition of good sense. It shall not be said that the sons of Montaigne, Voltaire, Renan . . .

SPECTATOR FROM BALCONY: Throw him out. Continue. (*The three knocks are sounded.*)

SCENE THREE

(*Same as the first scene. When Y pulls out his handkerchief, the second spectator stands:*)

SECOND SPECTATOR: Enough!

CRIES: Yes, enough, etc.

SECOND SPECTATOR: (*To his wife.*) Let's go.

(*They exit noisily but before leaving the auditorium, the second spectator shakes his fist at the stage.*)

SECOND SPECTATOR: It's shameful.

(*Tumult. The curtain falls. One hears cries of "Vive la France," "Continue," etc. One calls for the authors. Two actors bow in their stead. Curtain.*)

(The first three acts are translated by George Wellwarth and the last act by Annabelle Henkin Melzer.)

Free Entry

Roger Vitrac

(*Play in one act and seven scenes. The first three scenes and the last three are dreams; the fourth is the whole drama.*

First scene: Dream of Mr. Henry.
Second scene: Dream of Mr. William Roze.
Third scene: Dream of Mrs. Helen Roze.
Fifth scene: Dream of Mrs. Helen Roze.
Sixth scene: Dream of Mr. William Roze.
Seventh scene: Dream of Mr. Henry.

Mr. Henry takes the roles of the Man in Formal Dress, of Henry, of the Founding Child, of the Sailor, and of Mr. Henry.
Mr. William Roze takes those of the Sheep, of William, of the Policeman, of the Bather, and of the Restaurant Manager.
Mrs. Helen Roze takes those of the Rare Bird, of the Prostitute, of the Newspaper Vendor, and of the Waitress.

One could, in each scene, indicate the face of the dreamer. One ought preferably to separate the scenes by blackouts.)

CHARACTERS

The Man in Formal Dress
The Rare Bird
The Sheep
William
Henry
The Prostitute
A Woman in a Traveling Outfit (Mute Character)
Mr. William Roze
Mrs. Helen Roze
The Newspaper Vendor (Female)
The Policeman
The Foundling Child

The Bather
The Sailor
Mr. Henry
The Restaurant Manager
The Waitress

The scene takes place successively:
In a forest
By a lake
In a street
In a dining room
In a public square
By the sea
  and
In a restaurant

SCENE ONE

(A forest. Enter a Man in Formal Dress.)

MAN IN FORMAL DRESS: They invited me to dinner to strangle the children. Thanks a lot, that's not my dish. If that imbecile had not dressed up as a servant, I would still boast the excellence of a god so much the worse for my acquaintance. Woods of my childhood! It's odd the way one behaves nowadays. I left my boat on the other side of the lake but they've taught me to steal away. Hey there, this way, madame! The parapet at the end is carefully taken in every winter. I won't save you, the ice closes back over too quickly. Definitely my friend was wrong to get married. Hello Madame. *(Enter the Rare Bird.)*

THE RARE BIRD: Hello, William.

MAN IN FORMAL DRESS: She is deaf. *(Yelling.)* It is odd, madame, that you take me for the male parrot.

THE RARE BIRD: One thinks oneself in the middle of the belly. Myself, you know, William, I have aged a lot. When we were twenty, you had a horse which I never left. In the middle of the church I noticed that I was in my petticoat. No one paid attention to it, but you were red and you were saying: "It's the masons." They were at the door with bludgeons and I recognized among them your best friend: Henry.

MAN IN FORMAL DRESS: Useless to insist. I do not want to be taken for a cad. You will manage with William. You recognized me quite well. Me, my name is Henry. Goodbye.

THE RARE BIRD: Well then! In that case, you ought to remove your moustache. No hard feelings. Come to dinner tomorrow.

MAN IN FORMAL DRESS: But what kind of bird can this be? Glasses in hand. . . . Glasses in hand. The card hand passes. I've hit the jackpot.

SCENE TWO

(*By a lake. The Sheep, then The Man in Formal Dress.*)

THE SHEEP: (*Alone.*) Helen, what a funny idea to have bought that fur-lined coat. From the service staircase of the gamekeeper's house the grass is all straight. The earth is subject to little explosions. I didn't forget my revolver, I even tried to fire at a tree. The gun jammed. Helen ran away. But she loves to run in the fields. All the more so since I had to avoid the notary who wouldn't stop casting his fishing rod. (*Enter the Man in the Formal Dress.*)

MAN IN FORMAL DRESS: His death?

SHEEP: You are in mourning, Henry!

MAN IN FORMAL DRESS: They entrusted me to a child of six. I lost him that night. He climbed the hotel staircase. My mother spoke to me in a low voice and took him away. You will not refuse me this, she said to me; she was so good to me that I gave her my engineer's diploma and a bird which I was very fond of. How is Helen?

SHEEP: We waited for you last night. You didn't come. We preferred not to have dinner. Besides, the roast was burned and the maid obstinately kept opening the door and bursting into laughter. I reprimanded her a bit harshly. She answered me: "Madame has Monsieur and that's that." She's a good girl.

MAN IN FORMAL DRESS: I certainly intend to come to dinner.

SHEEP: My wife went near the fire. She absolutely wanted a peignoir of cotton batting, and since she wanted it blue, she put it on right away. I begged her not to burn the letters without showing them to me. She gave me a terrible fright. The peignoir caught fire and she fainted. Her first words were: "If I can't do anything now, I'll change underwear every day, and we'll see."

MAN IN FORMAL DRESS: You imagine things.

SHEEP: I haven't decided yet. The last time we went shopping, Helen disappeared at every moment. The saleswomen astonished me by offering all sorts of objects: gloves, perfumes, razors, feathers, brushes. Luckily a policeman put an end to that comedy. He took me into a corner, and since I refused to show him my papers, he yelled in my ear: "But just look at yourself!" I realized that I was crying bitter tears. Helen nudged me with her elbow. She wanted to go home. I saw that she had changed stockings. I commented about it. She answered me: "It's the fashion now." Besides there wasn't anyone in the elevator.

MAN IN FORMAL DRESS: It's always like that on Friday.

SHEEP: I gladly excuse you, but you should take your hands out of your pockets.

MAN IN FORMAL DRESS: (*Showing his hands.*) This? But these are pipes.

SHEEP: He's right, the beast. So much the better for you.

MAN IN FORMAL DRESS: Bah! I wear eyeglasses like everybody and I run faster than you. (*He runs away.*)

SHEEP: Robber! (*He makes as if to run after him but mistakes the direction and throws himself in the water.*)

SCENE THREE

(*Paris, in a narrow street, at night.*)

THE PROSTITUTE: (*Alone.*) It was a pretty room with flags on the walls. He had forced a blindfold over my eyes. He requested me to sit down and forgot me for a few instants. As he was turning around a table, I asked him what he had found. He returned with my mouth at his fingertips and put it back in place. He sat on my knees and unhooked my bodice behind my back. I remembered suddenly that my chemise was dirty. I begged him to let me alone. He did not insist and pointed out to me the odd design of his necktie. It was a green spiral where I don't know why the tick-tock of a watch could be heard. "Spain is not far," I thought. At that moment the door opened and a masked figure cried: "Morals squad." Immediately, undressed women sprang up from all the furniture. I followed them there. (*Enter William.*) Olives, olives, olives, olives.

WILLIAM: Have they harmed you?

PROSTITUTE: No sir. They advised me above all not to cross the street. This morning a child was run over. You see, there are still feathers in the mud.

WILLIAM: If you only knew what a hard time they're giving me.

PROSTITUTE: I haven't told you how their new apartment is arranged. There is an entrance with walls done in mirrors and bamboo. The living room connects with the kitchen which is also a bathroom. There is water on all the furniture and the bric-a-brac shelves are decorated with electric lamps. He was late in looking for the room which I didn't find.

I didn't dare ask them to open the back door. It was raining and I thought that you were waiting for me.

WILLIAM: No, I am coming back from my office. I was very busy. By the way, our friend Henry is dead.

PROSTITUTE: I know. It's the wicked women who killed him.

WILLIAM: You are better informed than I.

PROSTITUTE: Yes, aren't I? Aren't I? We, in our profession . . .

WILLIAM: So you don't want to? One hundred sous and the room?

PROSTITUTE: Swine! (*She bursts into sobs. Enter Henry, he is very pale. During the following dialogue, he speaks from a distance.*)

HENRY: You don't have to hold it against me.

PROSTITUTE: I don't hear you.

HENRY: First I thought of jumping out of the window, but on the balcony opposite was your rival who was waving to me. All of the inhabitants of the neighborhood had arranged to meet in front of the building to see me fall. One of them shouted: "Hands down." My valet reassured me. "It's the Protestants," he said. I found myself again in the middle of the boulevard where I learned, from a disheveled soldier, of your new profession.

PROSTITUTE: Well then! Mister Henry, we have ordered peach ice cream which you adore.

HENRY: That was a lot of trouble for nothing. I must leave on a trip.

PROSTITUTE: Far?

HENRY: That depends. Me, you know, I have something else to do.

PROSTITUTE: Business is business. (*Enter a Young Woman enveloped in a traveling coat. She is carrying a valise.*)

HENRY: Don't kill her, she has no hands. (*The Prostitute fires a revolver shot.*)

SCENE FOUR

(*A dining room. Mrs. Henry Roze is setting the table. Mr. William Roze reads his newspaper.*)

HE: Everything all right?

SHE: Everything's all right.

HE: Your head?

SHE: I took a pill.

HE: Take another one.

SHE: The doorbell.

HE: No. It's the telephone in the courtyard.

SHE: I have a kind of feeling . . .

HE: Helen! Please.

SHE: You'll see.

HE: Certainly he will come.

SHE: Obviously. (*Silence.*)

HE: Did you see?

SHE: No.

HE: They found a chronometer and a hat on the Pont des Arts.

SHE: Have they fished him out?

HE: No. (*Silence.*) Pass me my pipe.

SHE: You're not going to smoke now.

HE: Yes I am. (*The doorbell rings.*)

SHE: There, you see, it's not worth it. The doorbell.

HE: Pass me my pipe.

SHE: The doorbell.

HE: I tell you to pass me my pipe. (*The doorbell rings.*)

SHE: Oh! I'm going to open the door.

HE: God Almighty. (*Enter Mr. Henry who is leading Mrs. Helen Roze.*)

MR. HENRY: Hello William, everything all right?

MR. WILLIAM ROZE: All right, and you?

MRS. HELEN ROZE: Now then, let's eat. (*They sit down. Suddenly Mr. William Roze, who has his back to the audience, overturns the table. The lamp breaks. The scene is plunged into darkness. Pursuit. Cries: "Don't kill her. William. William. William. Help. Murderer. Murderer. Murderer."*)

SCENE FIVE

(*A public square.*)

NEWSPAPER VENDOR: (*She holds the Foundling Child by the hand.*) Knives, scissors . . . knives, scissors . . . knives, scissors . . . (*Enter the Policeman.*) It's me.

POLICEMAN: I ran away on a street which was transformed into a torrent. The passersby were crying: "He's burning, he's burning." But I had already put my uniform on and the automobile drivers who knew me greeted me grinning. They gave me a beautiful steel watch chain. Did you recognize me?

NEWSPAPER VENDOR: Oh! So many regiments pass by here.

POLICEMAN: I had to intervene in a matter where the examining magistrate didn't say a word without looking at me. Leaving his office he tapped my cheeks familiarly and said to me: "It's odd, isn't it?" I had slipped my left hand under my tunic, I couldn't get it back out again.

NEWSPAPER VENDOR: Have you read about the crime of the Daunou Street?

POLICEMAN: Ah! It's you. Well, then! Follow me.

NEWSPAPER VENDOR: Officer, they dragged me by the hair and my head bounced back at every step of the staircase. They abandoned me in a prairie. It was hot. The grass was all red. The other one hardly cared about me. He let the doctor go ahead. "Let them put her on ice," he said. Me, I had advised him to leave me the little boy. But the child never wanted to go fetch that fur which I had had the time to hide under the sheets.

POLICEMAN: Is he yours, this little boy?

FOUNDLING CHILD: You're not going to take her away? She's bleeding.

POLICEMAN: What's your name?

FOUNDLING CHILD: Henry, officer.

POLICEMAN: Ah . . . Henry, Henry, Henry, Henry . . . (*The Policeman thrashes the Newspaper Vendor and the Foundling Child.*)

SCENE SIX

(*At the seashore. A beach cabana.*)

THE BATHER: The hotels of this country are chalk white. Someone wrote on the wall of my room: "225 days to go." But why do they let animals free in the corridors? There is always someone who puts his hand on your shoulder as you go out. In the garden there is a woman whom one never sees except from behind. I pursued her a whole day. She seems to be looking for somebody.

THE SAILOR: Have you come for the season?

BATHER: You seem to me to be suspicious, you!

SAILOR: You are like white linen, William.

BATHER: I danced all night. It seemed to me that they were preparing something in the room next door. Travelers went out with a lit candle, hand in front of the flame. I found out. They answered me, turning away their heads, "that it would all be over soon."

SAILOR: Do you want to see your wife again, William?

BATHER: Ah! . . . (*Indicating the cabana.*) I am sure that she is getting undressed in there. If you'd seen her, she had grown. She must be naked now. (*The Bather moves toward the cabana.*)

SAILOR: Hey there! Where are you going, you?

BATHER: (*Opening the door of the cabana.*) Henry . . . look. (*A woman cut into pieces is in the cabana.*)

SCENE SEVEN

(*A restaurant.*)

MANAGER: (*To Mr. Henry, who enters.*) Hello, Mr. Henry, what can I serve you?

MR. HENRY: Scallops in the shell.

MANAGER: (*Calling.*) It will be scallops in the shell for Mr. Henry.

MR. HENRY: Tell me, where did you find that dish? (*He indicates the Waitress.*)

WAITRESS: Ah! (*She drops a pile of plates.*)

(Translated by Nahma Sandrow)

Handkerchief of Clouds

A Tragedy in Fifteen Acts

Tristan Tzara

Author's Introduction

This play was performed for the first time on May 17, 1924 at the Theatre de la Cigale as part of the "Soirees de Paris" organized by M. le Comte Etienne de Beaumont. (The author expresses his gratitude to the Count for the taste and subtle intelligence that was displayed in his production of *Handkerchief of Clouds*.)

The action takes place in a closed space, like a box, from which the actors cannot leave. All five sets are the same color. In the back, at a certain height, there is a screen that indicates where the action occurs, by means of reproductions blown up from illustrated post cards. These are rolled up on two rollers by a stagehand, who is visible at all times to the audience.

In the middle of the playing area there is a platform. To the right and the left are chairs, makeup tables, properties and the actors' costumes. The actors are on the set for the duration of the play. When they are not performing, they turn their backs to the audience, change costumes, or talk among themselves.

The primary action in each act takes place on the platform, while the Commentators operate in the playing area in front and to the side. At the end of each act, the lighting changes abruptly so that only the Commentators are lit; the actors then leave the stage. The lighting also changes abruptly at the end of each Commentary, when the light projectors light only the platform. The electricians and the reflectors are also visible.

Two stagehands bring on or take off the props from the stage. All the actors in the play keep their own names. In the present edition, the characters have the names of the actors who created their roles. The Poet, the Wife of the Banker and the Banker are the principal characters. A, B, C, D and E are the Commentators, who also play secondary roles.

Act One

(A Salon. Two armchairs, a telephone.)

THE POET: *(Seated. A valet hands him a letter. He reads it aloud.)* "Dear sir: Though the times are hard and not very propitious for adventure, and in spite of the omens that the Heavens send me every day in different forms, just like the rates of exchange and the values of the stock market of the heart, I still let myself write to you.

Your last book gives me confidence in you. I am not an unhappy woman; I am an empty woman. I have been married for three years. My husband is a banker; he is rich, handsome, young. I barely know him. He does not love me, I do not love him, we see each other very rarely. Perhaps it is his wealth and the attention it demands, or perhaps it is my own vital inadequacy, but I do not seem to be able to ensnare his interest which separates us and shuts us off from each other in a corset of indifferences. This is why I would like to see you. You will tell me, I hope, if these circumstances give me the right to fill my lungs with another breath than that for which the law destines me, lungs eager for affection." Sincerely, etc." *(He puts the letter in his pocket.)* Very interesting, very interesting. *(He telephones.)* . . . Elysee 44-33: M. Marcel Herrand is awaiting Mme. Andrea Pascal at his house. *(He calls out:)* Jean . . . if a lady arrives, show her in. *(Andrea enters.)*

THE POET: Please sit down, Madame. Your letter touched me, and the charm which your presence radiates adds itself to the brilliant burst of things that I love. And to make it clear from the start: I only love THINGS, their sparkle and their charm.

ANDREA: But how does one love *things*? I thought that *things* existed in order to manipulated . . . This, sir, must be more of your poetry.

THE POET: Yes, things exist in order to be manipulated, but with love. What do you want, I don't love men, I don't love women; I love *love*, that is to say, pure poetry.

ANDREA: Oh, sir, how you must have suffered in your life to a point of suppressing your passions in such a dull and uniform discipline. For I am sure that, in your heart of hearts, your emotions are as varied as the richness of colors, and that their combinations are more varied than the kaleidoscopic formations of submarine fauna.

THE POET: I have honestly cried so much that I have now arrived at a point where I can no longer distinguish between tears of sorrow and tears of joy.

ANDREA: What a tragedy these words express! My case is clear; it is not *my* unhappiness that I came to burden you with, for I am not like those other women who love to pour out their life stories to poets, who think of themselves as "misunderstood" . . . For the eagerness with which they present themselves to you often runs adrift under the guise of coquetry.

THE POET: I have arrived at last at a state at which I have leveled all sensations; an equilibrium which, even in the Spring, cannot submit to the love of another human being without being troubled. I am not empty, however. On the contrary. We might perhaps even look for a solution . . .

ANDREA: But do you believe that man can live alone, without ever putting himself out for another person in a reciprocal exchange of attractions and reactions? Do you really believe that man can live without loving?

THE POET: Perfectly, Madame, because happiness in this case would only be a sort of sickness; without this, one would never need periodically to take "lozenges of love" in order to arrive at a state of fulfillment, which is no more than a simulacrum, Madame. (*He stands up.*)

ANDREA: You would like to make me believe that you yourself are nothing more than a simulacrum, sir? (*She gets up.*)

THE POET: (*Taking her by the arm.*) When I was seventeen years old . . . (*They leave. Strike of the gong. Light change. The decor turns. During the Commentaries, the actors change costumes or makeup.*)

COMMENTARY

C: Where are they now, the poet and the woman whom he is discovering, like a clear note of a song on the edge of the road? They are in the process of dropping the stories of their lives like a rosary of pebbles that they let fall on the road in order to help them find their way back.

B: But soon it will be night and they will not be able to find the road that they marked with the pebbles, because the next day those pebbles will look just like all the others on the road, and everything will be thrown into confusion, the confusion which we try to escape from every day.

C: You are right, we can never turn back on the road of memory. On a bicycle or in an automobile, you can return to the point of departure, but always on another road than that on which memory has run. This road sinks into the heavy earth from which the daily bread of the mind is kneaded.

B: We are all sprinkled with pebbles. (*Lighting change.*)

Act Two

(*Venice.*)

THE FRIEND: Venice is somber at dusk. On the Grand Canal, the two rows of gold teeth of the palaces are the perfect distance for a smile proportioned to the dimensions of the city.

BANKER: I'm bored . . .

THE FRIEND: Why don't you simply learn how to appreciate this architecture in which pretension melts in liquid reflections?

BANKER: I'm bored . . .

THE FRIEND: What do you enjoy, my dear friend?

BANKER: I don't know. I'm bored. I'm going to leave this evening. Goodbye! (*The Banker leaves.*)

THE FRIEND: See you soon, I hope . . . (*The Poet and Andrea arrive in traveling clothes.*)

THE POET: (*To Andrea.*) I promised to take you everywhere to find your husband and to provoke a confrontation from which will explode the spark, telling us the direction we must follow in our cerebral investigations. I will be true to my word . . .

ANDREA: Now I feel more than confidence in you. I have renounced my will. As for finding my husband; I swear to you that . . .

THE FRIEND: (*Catching sight of Andrea.*) Oh! My dear woman, how are you? I am delighted to see you! I have just left your husband.

ANDREA: Where is he? Could you give me his address?

THE FRIEND: He was getting bored here, so he has just left for Monte Carlo. (*They leave. Strike of the gong. Change of set and lighting.*)

COMMENTARY

C: I think that Andrea loves Marcel, but she doesn't know it yet.

D: That would be sad, because the Poet does not love anyone; as he himself said, he loves only pure sensuality, which, through a play of subtleties, he calls poetry.

B: Don't make too much noise. Our heroes are probably trying to sleep in their first-class compartment that is leading them toward a destination still unknown. (*Lighting change.*)

Act Three

(*Train station.*)

STATIONMASTER: (*Walking, alone.*)
one after another the diffuse hours fall
on the tumors puffed up with memories and air
shorter or longer according to the boredom of the blood
prowling on the unstable launch over the snows
the pistils stretch out and suck the heart of the countryside
(*The train arrives: a Commentator imitates the noise of the train.*)

ANDREA: (*Enters, accompanied by her girlfriend.*) I am going to stop here. That is how I travel; I improvise my trip. But I don't see any station sign. Excuse me, sir, could you tell me the name of this place?

STATIONMASTER: You are in the "Peak of the Sentimental Consolidation," some miles from the border, 2,300 meters in altitude, on the thirty-seventh Meridian, pleasant climate, especially recommended by leading doctors to people who have nothing wrong with them. Strong alpine sensations. Winter sports. The "Peak of Sentimental Consolidation" is nicknamed the "Himalaya of the Poor."

ANDREA: It is charming! Could you show me to a hotel?

STATIONMASTER: Behind the train station, Madame, you will find the "Hotel de la Gare et des deux Terminus, Reunis": every modern comfort: hot and cold water, central heating, gas, telephone, electricity, bathrooms; moderate prices.

ANDREA: I like this place a great deal. Marcel will like it, too; I must tell him about it immediately.

GIRLFRIEND: This entire country has been painted by artists of the National! (*Strike of the gong. The two women leave. Set and lighting change.*)

COMMENTARY

A: It would be nice of you to pass my hat to me.

B: Do you have any lipstick?

C: I adore this play.

A: It wouldn't surprise me if it were a smash. (*Lighting change.*)

ACT FOUR

(*Monte Carlo.*)

1st MAN: So it's true that the Banker lost his entire fortune yesterday evening?

2nd MAN: Perfectly true, vast sums of money. But, judging from the information I received this morning, this wipeout will not involve the money of his clients.

1st MAN: But all of his personal fortune?

2nd MAN: And that of his wife.

1st MAN: As for what he gave his wife . . . You know, they never see each other . . . there are rumors . . .

2nd MAN: It is he approaching? Let's not give him the impression that we know anything about his misfortune, for often this type of tragedy, by the mere fact that it has been made public, and is a topic of interest in conversation, can drive its suffering victim to abandon the weak life that still animates his carcass.

1st MAN: And in order to avoid a scandal, his corpse would seriously risk being dumped into one of those drawers that ornament the rocks near here, like a letter which a guilty wife hides as soon as she hears someone breathing.

BANKER: (*Enters, in high spirits.*) Well, my friends, have you heard the news? I am happy and full of hope.

1st MAN: You have hope of regaining your fortune?

BANKER: None at all; I am happy to have lost it. It was weighing heavily on my veins. Now I am happy and full of hope.

1st MAN: Oh!

2nd MAN: How is this possible?

BANKER: It is only now that I have become rich. (*The Banker exits.*)

1st MAN: I believe he has evil intentions; perhaps he thinks that the money with which his clients had entrusted him would be enough to . . .

2nd MAN: No . . . they have all withdrawn their money. I believe, rather that this throw of the dice has mixed madness with his reason. (*Strike of the gong. They leave. Change of lighting and sets.*)

COMMENTARY

A: Why don't they understand that the *content* of a word is not necessarily related to its sound? The Banker says: "I am rich" when he is poor, because he was poor when he was rich. He is rich with life, now that the wallet of his heart is no longer encumbered with innumerable visiting cards that destiny deposits with bitterness on persons who, never being at home, are constantly causing traffic jams of the spirit on the principal arteries of the city and of memory.

B: And it was the casino that rendered this great service to him, by lifting off all that which, without his knowing it, was troubling him deeply.

ACT FIVE

(A garden. Andrea and the Poet are seated on a bench.)

ANDREA: What do you think of this letter?

POET: What does he say at the end?

ANDREA: His words are: "Since I have rediscovered my natural wealth . . . "

POET: That is to say, since he lost his artificial poverty . . .

ANDREA: Yes, in other words, his money. "Since I have rediscovered my natural wealth, I think only of you; I breathe in fresh air, which I have not known for many long years. It seems that I am on the threshold of a new life. Until tomorrow, etc." It is very general, but you do understand what he wants, don't you? I am afraid of it suddenly, and I don't know why. Before, when I didn't see him, I was calmer. And since you have arrived at the "Peak of the Sentimental Consolation" . . . There is a secret that I must tell you, Marcel, which you never suspected.

POET: That can wait. First we should find out what his intentions are.

ANDREA: They certainly will be honorable, but even that will not be a solution to this crisis . . . because I have neglected to tell you that this secret of mine begins to give a flavor to the void I used to feel; it is no longer empty . . .

POET: Solution . . . solution . . . there is never a solution; either you do things or you don't, and the result is always the same: you drop dead in the end.

ANDREA: Nevertheless, I would also like to benefit from the carelessness of those who do not perceive that time passes with painful slowness.

POET: *(Looking at his watch.)* He is going to arrive in a few moments. Indeed, this sudden change in the mind of a man who felt nothing but indifference and emptiness toward his wife, strikes me as disturbing but most interesting. *(The Banker arrives.)*

ANDREA: Mr. Marcel Herrand, let me present my husband . . .

ALIBI: *(Arrives.)* The necklace has been found!

BANKER: Necklaces are made to be found.

POET: *(To Andrea.)* They are finding all the necklaces.

ANDREA: Even those that had never been lost. *(The Banker leads Andrea into a corner of the garden.)*

ALIBI: (*To the Poet.*) Allow me to introduce myself: Mac Alibi, detective: enquiries, indiscretions, quick divorces, rehabilitations, anonymous letters, surveillance and intuition.

BANKER: What must you conclude from this conversation? I love you . . .

ANDREA: After years of waiting and solitude, I need some time to think this over. (*They kiss.*)

ALIBI: Excuse me, an urgent affair calls me to Martinique.

POET: There is nothing left for me to do but follow you—wait for me, I'm leaving with you.

ANDREA: (*Running after the Poet.*) Why are you leaving so quickly . . . Are you thus abandoning me? What am I going to do all alone? . . .

POET: It's for the best. I'm leaving, I'm dying a little . . . Solitude will teach you to live.

ANDREA: But why so quickly, so quickly . . . I would like you to have a memento . . . What can I give you? . . . Take this black velvet half-mask, souvenir of the masked ball—in the middle of which you taught me to live a life contrary to that which I had in me.

POET: Life, it is so strangely disguised, life . . . happily, it is of no importance. Good-bye! (*The Poet leaves with Alibi.*)

ANDREA: (*To the Banker.*) He has gone . . .

BANKER: (*To the Poet.*) Bon Voyage! . . . (*Strike of the gong. They exit. Set and lighting change.*)

COMMENTARY

POET: (*Getting dressed.*) Let us fit ourselves out for the needs of the sea and the Tropics. All aboard for adventure! Voyages fill the suitcases of the heart, which the Poet always holds open for the demands of chance and the fleeting necessities of the hour.

B: You who have traveled so often, Staquet, what do you do in order to avoid being bored?

C: Well, I travel.

A: Do you think that Herrand is traveling because he was getting tired of Andrea?

D: I myself am unable to come to any conclusion.

E: Me either.

C: That is the reason this play is badly made. Even though we are the Commentators, that is to say, the subconscious of the drama, the playwright never even let *us* know why the Poet does not love Andrea.

E: Yet she is pretty and intelligent; you are aware that I know her very well myself.

B: The fact that you act the role of Andrea's friend on stage does not give you the right to believe that you are her friend in real life.

A: But she could easily be his friend outside this dramatic action, this play, in real life, in her own life—how would you know?

C: Oh! There is nothing so tedious as these endless discussions on the difference between theatre and reality! (*Lighting change.*)

ACT SIX

(*The sea. The Poet, the Captain and Alibi are standing, holding before them a canvas that depicts the deck of a ship. Each man has a glass of wine in his hand. Heroic postures.*)

POET: Captain! The wine is good.

CAPTAIN: Because it sweetens the bitter foreboding of anguish when an adventure approaches its consummation.

ALIBI: Captain! The sea is vast.

CAPTAIN: But safe when you know how to glide between the gelatinous and marvelously moving bumps.

POET: Captain! Do you know women?

CAPTAIN: Woman: she is far, she is always far away, and it is only distance that attracts and ties her to you.

ALIBI: Captain! Do you know what death is?

CAPTAIN: Of all dangers, it is the worst, let us say, because it is impossible to imagine the abrupt end of consciousness, which sets in motion the wristwatch and time.

POET: Captain, you are right!

CAPTAIN: The wind, storms, the ashes of songs, the confidence of my men, the idea of sacrifice and danger, have sprinkled my reason with the germs of Springtime.

ALIBI: Captain! The sun is soft.

CAPTAIN: But hard when it slows the blood of the workers.

POET: Captain: I have a heavy heart.

CAPTAIN: Like the slowed blood of the workers remembering the sun.

ALIBI: Captain, I'm hungry!

CAPTAIN: Me, too! (*Strike of the gong. They leave carrying the boat. Set and lighting change.*)

COMMENTARY

C: Let's travel back in time now.

D: Like the movies do.

A: What did Andrea do when the Poet left?

C: We are about to see.

B: Lower the tulle curtain!

E: The curtain of memory! (*The tulle curtain falls.*)

D: This scene takes place in Andrea's apartment.

A: The vagueness of the objects is not that of the dream. It indicates only that this scene does not occur in a normal progression of time, within the logical sequence of the acts.

(*Lighting change.*)

ACT SEVEN

(*A boudoir, behind the tulle curtain.*)

ANDREA: He has gone, and forever.

GIRL FRIEND: Nothing is certain.

ANDREA: I am going to tell you my secret. I am in love with Marcel, and I have loved him from the first day I saw him.

GIRL FRIEND: Why didn't you ever say anything to him?

ANDREA: What good would it have done? He didn't love me . . . he didn't love anyone, you know that . . . His eyes are full of the nimbleness of dangerous acts. I am suffering . . . it is too late, his image has already wormed its way into the shadow of my heart. More and more I find myself believing in his perfection; it is that which can give rise to supreme indifference. He made his indifference transcend every act, because, even though his spirit was constantly moving, he coated each gesture with a layer of indifference, like Time burying an event by covering it with veils of forgetfulness.

GIRL FRIEND: Andrea, you know how much I like you; but I don't understand why you kept trying to find your husband . . .

ANDREA: I don't know any more myself; I was thrown from one event to the next like a tennis ball, and I don't understand anything. It was he, Marcel, who kept insisting . . . Jacques kissed me when he arrived; Marcel probably thought that *that* could make up for the miserable mass of shapeless desires which crowded the void of my heart.

GIRL FRIEND: But Jacques loves you, that's some consolation. Maybe with time . . .

ANDREA: Nothing, nothing will help. I am alone, completely alone. He is far away, and I will never see him again . . . (*She cries.*)

BANKER: (*Arrives.*) Well! What's happening here? Another crisis? . . . Andrea, calm yourself. Don't you realize that my tenderness knows no obstacles?

GIRL FRIEND: I must be going now. Goodbye, Andrea. Jacques is right, love is a duty like any other. It is nothing interesting . . . It builds its nest wherever you tell it to . . . and it appears in the corner that you prepare for it. All the rest is romanticism. Goodbye, Andrea.

ANDREA: Come see me tomorrow.

BANKER: The concept of reality to which you have just alluded, Miss Romée, will save Europe; better sentimental crises than economic crises. (*Strike of the gong. They leave. Set and lighting change.*)

COMMENTARY

B: Raise the curtain of memory! (*The curtain rises.*)

A: Let us now return to the other reality, to true reality, the reality of the handkerchief of clouds.

D: Since it is the middle of the play, don't you think an intermission would go well here?

C: No, the author did not want any intermission. He says that it is the intermission which has killed the theatre.

D: Then let's continue.

A: On stage for the eighth Act, on stage for the eighth . . . on stage for the eighth . . .

B: OK, OK, everyone's ready.

D: Did you see him? He's in the room.

E: That is unimportant, you will find your places, I'm sure.

D: Everything will turn out all right.

B: Almost everything.

D: Why "almost?" . . . Rhetorical precautions! I am positive: *Everything* will turn out . . .

B: Here is the secret of success: be positive, be wrong, but always be it with authority and you will succeed.

E: Only if "to succeed" means to fool yourself, to steal from yourself parts of your own individuality.

C: What philosophers!

A: On stage for the eighth, on stage for the eighth. Your discussion will not hold up before the hurricane, which will break loose later in the drama unfolding here. (Lighting change.)

ACT EIGHT

(An island, represented by several paintings of plantations, Negroes, etc. . . . combined to form a tableau.)

COLONIAL GENTLEMEN: *(Explaining to the Poet and Alibi with a walking stick in his hand.)* No longer must the Negro take on oversized burdens; he can leave them on the back of civilization. The plow is drawn by two oxen. What is an ox? An ox is an animal, usually white, who tolerates all sorts of vicissitudes—not because it lacks the gift of language—but mainly because it is too busy chewing its cud, which constitutes its nourishment. But let us return to our subject. What do these Negroes transport? They transport tobacco. Tobacco is a plant with green leaves, as the sky is blue. That's where the expression comes from, to get severely beaten, you will be green as hope.

Huge hairdressers with enormous scissors clip the countryside. The harvests usually are excellent on account of the rain and the beautiful weather that are our best friends. The leaves of the tobacco plant are scattered everywhere, like bank notes, through the motion of a sower. They dry out in a natural fashion. The leaves are turned into tobacco by workers in civilian or native dress. Rolled and stuck together, they form cigars; cut in the shape of macaroni, they become cigarettes; and ground at the mill, they become snuff, extremely popular now.

The planters are rich men, and the colored people are well brought up. You can see all of this on this tableau. An anonymous society is being formed for the purpose of roasting the corpses of the colored people, who, because of the rain, are becoming more and more abundant; then the plan is to grind them up and sell the product under the name "colored powder." It can be used by women, who will either pat it with light tissues over the surface of the skin, or inhale it through the nasal passages. It is not necessary to understand the slave charm to guess that this substance is made of GOLD, and that the gold of this substance seems to have the same effects and efforts as real gold; therefore, as is the case with all gold substances, it will earn a great deal of money. *(Strike of the gong. They leave. Set and lighting change.)*

COMMENTARY

A: Alibi, after going to the bank where he verifies his account, puts on a false nose and moustache, and sets out in pursuit of the thief. This jewel thief is very famous. Alibi will surely discover him among the rich planters or among the workers, for his nose is good. *(Each Commentator, in speaking his reply, moves in front of the stage. They form a tight group. They appear to follow the Poet into the room.*)

B: The Poet is looking for a hotel.

A: He finds one.

C: He checks in.

D: Now he is sad.

A: His sorrow grows greater and greater.

B: It lays its massive hand on his body.

A: But his body, alas, has become very weak.

B: Ever since it suffered the terrible jolts that the sea inflicted on him, while the boat was sliding between the gelatinous humps, etc. . . . . as the Captain so delicately phrased it.

A: The Poet is suffering.

B: Yes, he suffers, but he still does not know why.

A: But we know it well!

C: Because he will not be with his fantasy for long,

B: to make navigable in a pure path

A: his pain, without cause or effect.

C: Here he is!

A: He is on the seashore.

B: He is walking.

C: He stops and sighs.

B: He makes a gesture which signifies "Courage!"

E: He says, "too bad,"

A: and walks toward the forest. (*They remain standing, and group themselves on the two sides of the stage in order to listen to the monologue. Lighting change.*)

ACT NINE

(*A forest. On the set is written in large letters: MONOLOGUE.*)

THE POET: (*Advances with a velvet half-mask in his hand.*) To live, to die. To the right, to the left. Standing up, lying down. In front, behind. Above, below. Why these gymnastics about an evil that has nothing to do with the body? I love her . . . Yes, miserably, and from what a distance! The islands have so many surprises in store for me, the islands, these unexpected flats rising out of the blue waves, on which eager fantasy flings herself for want of other more carnal satisfactions. And my heart is an enormous restaurant where the entire world eats to its heart's content, without paying the bill or the ten percent tip. But to what end? I would like to be able to tear open the meninges of my brain like the inside of a toy, in order to see the mechanism of my love for her. I, who

have never loved. (*He puts on the mask.*)
    Love which in fine and pure circumstances
knocked with such subtle regrets my days my nights
on the closed doors of time with gentle taps
which do not wake the travelers in hotels
and for which I believed myself widower, for which I was in mourning,
which I believed wrenched from my middle-aged breast
and carried far, far away, by the virile and rude
current of the nuptial mud, rapid and volcanic,
comes today to disturb the calm hypothesis
similar to the magic wine which ferments in the cellar
in the depths of my slow head and my solitude.
The night, like a plug, was closing off the large pipe
out of which the day leaks, the luxury of its light;
the lives, little and big, alternatively,
still felt the dream and the sleep another time
to weigh the black antique smoke on the scale
of their eyelids, docile and heavy with songs.
But I, full of the sound left by her words,
—of the erased prints of footsteps in the desert
which was my destiny the day when I first saw her—
vibrant as her word at the sound of memory,
I was standing here, trying to measure
the residue of time which memory deposits
along its journey, slices of rare words,
perspectives of fleeting and artful images
to grind these hard and heavy grains into thoughts:
flour of the brain, dust of this world.
Sand, if the wind troubles its clarity,
blinds the cheerfulness of the humble pedestrians,
and the thought, also rolling around itself,
hides the fruit and the lie for you from the whirlwind.
Thus I remain, a piece of flotsam from the daily shipwreck.
Love covers the eyes of my heart and mind.
Rapacious fish, the monsters of the clouds,
the hatreds, the pains, the crises, the horrors,
the vices, the germs and the evil spirits,
all strike me, humiliate me, bite me and tear
the prepared behavior with its propitious cares
which I was supposed to carry this evening to the ball at the Opera.
And all of this for two blue eyes
and for the five o'clock tea which dusk offers to the
Spring in porcelain cups, invisible

as the stars.
(*He hums the "Violettera." The orchestra picks up the air, muted, and continues to play it through the middle of Act Ten. He leaves. Set and lighting change.*)

COMMENTARY

(*The Commentators resume their places.*)

B: His song was very beautiful. It was also authentic, seeing as how it was from South America.

A: You are always frivolous.

C: But he is right, since it is a question of the poetic, or rather, the human value, in which the Poet has dressed his despair. I am speaking about the moment after he put the mask on his face, to hide from himself the implausible side of a similar language.

B: As for me, you know, I believe in nothing.

C: Thus nothing can have any importance; you can say "rubber" and think "chrysanthemum." Where are we going, where are we going? Ask that instead of congratulating yourself on such a pure and classic effort in which we are permitted to participate.

B: As for me, you know, I believe in nothing.

A: Then be quiet, for your skepticism is sterile. Put yourself in his place: *he needs* to take poetry as reality, and reality as an illusion.

B: As for me, if I hadn't known at the beginning how the author was going to end this play, I would not hesitate for a moment in proclaiming that poetry is a negligible product of latent madness, and that it is not in the least necessary for the onward march of civilization and progress.

A: But that is not the problem, and we do not have time to discuss it. (*Lighting change.*)

ACT TEN

(*A restaurant. The Friend and the Captain arrive and sit down at a table.*)

FRIEND: And this trip?

CAPTAIN: Well, a stormy sea almost every day. Marcel Herrand crossed the Equator for the first time, and his baptism was very lively.

FRIEND: Listen: on the subject of Marcel Herrand, just this minute as I was opening this newspaper, my eyes happened to fall on an extremely curious article.

CAPTAIN: An article?

FRIEND: No; rather a poetic fantasy. I am almost positive that our hero hides under the psuedonym "telephone." I will read some passages to you: "The wind dances on tiptoe over the sea. With pointed fingers it lifts the handkerchiefs of the waves stretching to the sun. It combs the water. It paints it blue. It washes the sea."

CAPTAIN: It's very beautiful, but it's useless. Would you pass me the newspaper? (*He reads:*) "The mountains receive a packet of chocolate. The mountains are behind young girls who are grouped together on the staircase. The windows are still open. At their feet you see baskets of flowers and a watchdog. The dog does not bark; he is pensive. The young girl in the middle, standing on a stool, holds a sealed letter in her right hand. Her left hand rests on the shoulder of one of her sisters. They are well-behaved . . ."

FRIEND: Do you know what this makes me think of? A long time ago, when I was in Italy, I met a famous singer who made one's blood boil with her voice and its innumerable capitulations. I was never able to understand the purpose of this strange occupation.

C: (*Standing on a chair, cries out:*) —The Poet, in the throes of his love, or his love plain and simple, returns to Paris, continually hiding his plots and intentions, and invites the prodigal spouses out to dinner at a chic restaurant.

CAPTAIN: Let's leave them their place.

FRIEND: Let's resume our role as Commentators. (*They leave. The music grows louder. The Maître D'Hôtel and the Groom walk up on the stage, from behind, to the right and left of the table. The Poet, Andrea, and the Banker enter and are seated. The music stops.*)

POET: There I was on a cliff. The sun, once more before disappearing, was gathering its wrinkles of light . . .

ANDREA: Oh, it's exquisite, it's exquisite . . .

POET: There I was on the cliff . . . In the distance I could hear the sounds of farm machinery, like rattling chains, which, during the day, had imprisoned men in fear of the day to come, crowded together under the shed. The day was coming to an end . . .

BANKER: Ah! How I wish I could have been there!

POET: There I was on the cliff . . . When suddenly, in an unprecedented burst of light, frightening in its paleness, a beast, a beast . . .

ANDREA: (*A shout.*) My God! Something terrible is going to happen to him . . .

BANKER: Be reasonable, Andrea, he is sitting right by our sides . . .

POET: . . . a beast, an enormous beast, suddenly appeared in front of me. It moved slowly because it was advancing with uncertainty. I realized—needless to say that I was still on the cliff—I realized that each second could cut short or even terminate my vital instinct. So I picked up my rifle, and with just one shot, I killed it.

ANDREA & BANKER: (*Applauding.*) Very good . . . very good . . .

POET: A large breath, but not a strident one. A breath of death and certainty. My curiosity returned; with all possible caution I drew closer, and . . .

ANDREA: What was it?

BANKER: Tell us, what?

POET: . . . and I found an enormous, an immense—the climate and the eccentricity of such a distant country, alone, could produce such a large—

BANKER: Come on, tell us: what was it?

ANDREA: What was it that you killed?

POET: It was a flower . . . (*A little time passes . . . exaggerated and silly laughter from the Commentators. Exclamations: "That is poetry!" . . . "a flower" . . . "it's not funny," etc. . . .*) With the aid of Alibi, who was still in the country, I undertook an investigation. The flower had been known on the island for many years. They called it "The Troglodyte."

ANDREA: What an enchanted land! It seems to me that I have always lived in blood, sensuality and . . . flowers. You are a poet, you understand me . . .

POET: You can not even suspect how true that is; if you only knew . . . (*He stands up, assumes a tragic air.*) . . . if you only knew . . . The check, please. (Strike of the gong. They leave. Set and lighting change.)

COMMENTARY

E: They are going to the theatre.

B: Here you could insert a very nice problem of general order:
To what point the truth is true.
To what point the lie is false.
To what point the truth is false.
To what point the lie is true.
(*Lighting change.*)

ACT ELEVEN

(*The Avenue of the Opera.*)

POET: Do you like jewels?

ANDREA: I adore them.

BANKER: No, I don't like them very much; what about you?

POET: Me? . . .

ANDREA: Jewels are the bonbons that we offer in the evening to soften it for us.

POET: Their reflections are the needles that women stick in the flesh of the imagination.

BANKER: I know that you dearly love dresses and fine fabrics.

ANDREA: Oh! I adore them.

POET: That doesn't surprise me; you're very chic.

BANKER: Fabrics become one with the skin by the intermediary of lace, and lengthen the lines of the body.

POET: Yes, when it is not a marriage of reason, they extend them and give them the *feeling* of lines which meet in infinity.

ANDREA: The figure before everything!

POET: No, the feeling.

BANKER: I prefer color. (*Andrea and the Banker leave.*)

POET: (*Aside.*) It is strange, very strange. They do not even suspect the anxiety which scatters my actions in the wind, and which, this evening at the theatre, will peel off the rind of confusion which imprisons the orange of their sinister existence. (*Strike of the gong. He leaves. Set and lighting change.*)

COMMENTARY

A: Pardon me, but I don't understand at all what our heroes are doing on the Avenue of the Opera.

E: I have already told you, they are going to the theatre.

D: It is not absolutely necessary that they go by the Avenue of the Opera.

C: Actually, that is true; this scene could have been represented in a more abstract fashion.

B: Here you could insert a very nice problem of general order:
At what point the truth is true

C : At what point the lie is false.

D : At what point the truth is false.

E : At what point the lie is true.

ANDREA: First of all, I forbid you to discuss the emotions which, being addressed to me in a manner that was as direct as it was public, take on dramatic and substantial meanings in Marcel's mouth. I forbid you to ask, or even discuss, if I loved Marcel or my husband; the conclusion of your discussion might have, perhaps for a second, a passing truth, in relation to a brilliant or banal phrase; but such a conclusion would not carry any weight unless I myself approve it.

A: Permit me to protest, Madame, for it is more than possible that you yourself do not know what you wish; but we, removed from the action, can understand the will of the Gods who rule us.

C: That is called free will.

B: That which determines the results of boxing matches.

D: We are the words of God, we walk on earth and we intermingle like the words of God in elegant phrases, but stripped of the meaning which rules us.

B: From time to time we receive punches in the jaw. These are the words which God sends us so we remember Him.

D: But beware, my friend, for it is probably in vain to count to nine; his knockout will be an obscurity more final than blackness or night.

A: I am returning to the beginning of our conversation: What are they going to do at the theatre?

C: (*Advances.*) All right, I'll explain it all to you: *Hamlet* is playing. This production is a mousetrap and a surprise. It is the Poet who is the surprise, and who plays Hamlet. You will ask me why; but that is the mystery of the drama. The intelligent public will discover the key on the following day.

D: (*Getting up on a chair.*) —With this key you will be able to open everything, for the key is an egg; the Egg comes from the Dove, Columbus discovered America, America has plantations of dollars, dollars set the tone, the tone is a pitch of the violin, and the violin is by Ingres. (*Lighting changes.*)

ACT TWELVE

(*The ramparts of Elsinore.*)

POLONIUS: How now, Ophelia, what's the matter?

OPHELIA: Oh, my Lord, my Lord, I have been so affrighted!

POLONIUS: With what, i' the name of God?

OPHELIA:
My Lord, as I was sewing in my closet,
Lord Hamlet, with his doublet all un-braced,
No hat upon his head, his stockings fouled,
Ungartered and down-gyved to his ankle,
Pale as his shirt, his knees knocking each other,
And with a look so piteous in purport,
As if he had been loosed out of hell
To speak of horrors—he comes before me.

POLONIUS: Mad for thy love?

OPHELIA: My Lord, I do not know, But truly do I fear it.

POLONIUS: What said he?

OPHELIA:

He took me by the wrist and held me hard;
Then goes he to the length of all his arm,
And with his other hand thus o'er his brow,
He falls to such perusal of my face
As he would draw it. Long stayed he so.
At last, a little shaking of mine arm,
And thrice his head thus waving up and down,
He raised a sigh so piteous and profound
As it did seem to shatter all his bulk
And end his being. That done, he lets me go:
And with his head over his shoulder turned,
He seemed to find his way without his eyes,
For out o' doors he went without their help,
And to the last bended their light on me.

(*Exit Ophelia. Enter Hamlet.*)

POLONIUS: How does my good Lord Hamlet?

HAMLET: Well, God-a-mercy.

POLONIUS: Do you know me, my Lord?

HAMLET: Excellent well. You are a fishmonger.

POLONIUS: Not I, my Lord.

HAMLET: Then I would you were so honest a man.

POLONIUS: Honest, my Lord?

HAMLET: Aye, sir. To be honest, as this world goes, is to be one man picked out of ten thousand.

POLONIUS: That's very true, my Lord.

HAMLET: For if the sun breeds maggots in a dead dog, being a good kissing carrion—Have you a daughter?

POLONIUS: I have, my Lord.

HAMLET: Let her not walk i' the sun. Conception is a blessing, but as your daughter may conceive, friend, look to 't.

POLONIUS: How say you by that? (*Aside.*) Still harping on my daughter . . . What do you read, my Lord?

HAMLET: Words, words, words.

POLONIUS: (*Aside.*) Though this be madness, yet there is method in 't. Will you walk out of the air, my Lord?

HAMLET: Into my grave.

POLONIUS: Indeed, that's out of the air. (*Aside.*) —My honorable Lord, I will most humbly take my leave of you.

HAMLET: You cannot, sir, take from me anything that I will more willingly part withal—except my life, except my life, except my life. (*Exit

Polonius.)
I have heard that guilty creatures sitting at a play
Have by the very cunning of the scene
Been struck so to the soul that presently
They have proclaimed their malefactions.

(*Enter Polonius.*)

POLONIUS: My Lord, the Queen would speak with you, and presently.
HAMLET: Do you see yonder cloud that's almost in the shape of a camel?
POLONIUS: By the mass, and 'tis like a camel, indeed.
HAMLET: Methinks it is like a weasel.
POLONIUS: It is backed like a weasel.
HAMLET: Or like a whale.
POLONIUS: Very like a whale.
HAMLET: Than I will come to my mother by and by . . .
POLONIUS: I will say so. (*Exit Polonius.*)
HAMLET:
'By and by' is easily said . . . now could I drink hot blood
And do such bitter business as the day
Would quake to look on.

(*Strike of the gong. Set and lighting change.*)

COMMENTARY

A: Night is now complete in the mind of the Poet, for the jewels ring in their little bells and the flower sinks into the soft matter of mushrooms.

What did he want? He was hoping that the hook of his lie would thus catch the carp of the truth. He took the Banker and his wife to the theatre to catch them in the mousetrap. The mousetrap is Hamlet. But the Poet is mistaken, because the Banker is the legal spouse of Andrea. It was, moreover, their first and last marriage. We saw that the Poet was neither Andrea's son nor the Banker's nephew; actually, here is what happened:

At the price of the illusion of the island, the Poet brought back the phantom of the first love which Andrea felt for him. That is to say:
1) Andrea was in love with the Poet;
2) the Poet was not in love with her;
3) as soon as he left for the island, the Poet began to fall in love with Andrea;
4) having returned to Paris, he realized that Andrea did not love him any more;
5) she was in love with the Banker;

6) thus the love of Andrea is the phantom;

7) the love of Marcel is the illusion of the island.

As a consequence: at the price of the illusion of the island, the Poet brought back the phantom of the first love which Andrea felt for him.

He is thus himself the phantom, and wishes to take his revenge. The usurper is the Banker. But, since the Poet is nothing but a phantom, (because he was in love with Andrea in the form of the illusion of the island), he can do nothing by himself, and must leave the responsibility to Hamlet. Not having the time to search, and also by "economy, economy," the phantom becomes one with Hamlet. Thus at the same time the Poet is both the phantom and Hamlet. He plays both roles. It is the only explanation that one could give to the fishhook lie, for there are no others, given that the Banker and his wife are a very respectable family, carp of the truth, and are not in any way related to either the worm-eaten King or Queen of Denmark. (*Lighting change.*)

ACT THIRTEEN

(*A street. The night. A street lamp. Two Apaches enter. Whistles.*)

C : A man walks in the garden of crises
  with his cane he beats the wind in
  the windmill of the dreams of day.
  (*The Banker enters and walks across the stage.*)
C: He demonstrates the carnal advantage of the exquisite hour
 Placed with brightness on the brightness of his placing and of his day.
  (*The Apaches assassinate the Banker and drag his body offstage. Silence. A whistle.*)
E: Curses, curses! (*Two Agents walk across the stage. Strike of the gong. Set and lighting change.*)

COMMENTARY

J: Was it a simple or complex murder of the drama of jealousy? Would Hamlet have killed the Banker? (*Lighting change.*)

ACT FOURTEEN

(*A library. On the set is written in large letters: TWENTY YEARS LATER.*

Andrea is seated in an armchair, her two children standing on her right and left.)

ANDREA: Ever since the demon of his attractiveness dissolved like candy melting in my mouth, I have felt tranquility slide its comfortable pillow under my head.

FIRST CHILD: But tell me, Mother, did the Poet have any talent?

ANDREA: I can assure you that I never understood much of what he used to write . . . But then, he wrote much less than he thought, since he wished to live his poetry.

SECOND CHILD: Obviously you understood his life as little as his poetry.

ANDREA: They found the corpse of your father in the street, lying next to one of those red lanterns which the pavers light near their work, during the night, to attract the attention of the cars and passersby.

FIRST CHILD: Indeed, the work of the murderer was very refined. He was hoping, if I might express it thus, that no accident would ever befall him.

ANDREA: It was not the Poet who did it, it wasn't him, I'm positive about that. His feelings were more noble.

SECOND CHILD: True, because if it were the Poet who killed him, why would the Poet have hidden his love from Mother, *after* as well as before the murder?

FIRST CHILD: I myself do not trust poetry. For me it is a convenient form, a mundane form of madness.

In its name one can dare anything. Furthermore, it is not in the least necessary to the onward march of civilization and progress.

ANDREA: (*Dreamily.*) He was so noble, so great, so pure, so good . . .

SECOND CHILD: Who are you talking about, Mother, the Poet or the Banker? (*Strike of the gong. They leave. Set and lighting change.*)

COMMENTARY

C:

Time flows flows flows
Time flows flows flows
Time flows flows flows flows
Time flows flows flows flows flows
drop by drop
drop drop by drop drop
drop drop drop by drop drop drop
drop drop drop drop by drop drop drop drop.

D:

A chinese torture
drop by drop

flows flows
fills the pockets of reason
which the tailor of God left without bottom
(what negligence)
with drops of gold, silver of time
and puts before us the problem of general order that we know
the refreshed course of blood in the hunt
the refreshed animal hunted by the blood
the hunt for blood of the infinite animal which runs.
That is what we can blow in the face of the unfurled sails
of time traveling over inexpressible seas
on the boat with unfurled and everlasting
sails like the water and the weather
which pass over the boat with unfurled
sails traveling over inexpressible waters.
(*Lighting change.*)

ACT FIFTEEN

(*A garret. On the set is written in large letters: TWENTY YEARS LATER.*)

THE POET: (*Seated at a table.*) Let's add a little more confusion to these acts; but graciously and ironically. Hamlet (*he laughs*). Let's be concise (*he goes through the motion of catching a fly*). A fly is clear and ironic without knowing it. It irritates my colleagues, that is to say, the whole world. But it is not conscious of this. Let us act with a clear conscience, knowing in advance what is going to happen to us. Or, on the contrary, let us travel on the stream of the unexpected and our instincts. The Banker is dead, assassinated, but he did not know it. He was like the fly: he did not know that he was going to trouble the memory that he left behind in the life of Andrea.

Who killed the Banker? I know who. If you consciously push madness to the extreme, you will be less mad than the others.

CONCIERGE: (*Enters.*) Ah, ah, my good man, I am at the age when one always prefers walking down the stairs to walking up. It is difficult. Here is your mail.

POET: Thank you, thank you. You remember the plays we used to act in together?

CONCIERGE: Oh, all of that is so long ago. Goodbye, sir, until tomorrow. (*The Concierge leaves.*)

A: That's what became of Ophelia.

B: The lake in which she tried to drown herself froze over with death and terror at the approach of her innocent apparition.

A: She never could find shelter anywhere except near the heater in a vacant concierge's room.

POET: And the great festival in which the spirit exerts itself during the sweet struggles of rhyme and of love, takes on this evening an ending as unprecedented as it is unpraiseworthy for the audience, by a tragic explosion; and of which the consequences will forever strike the clouds with daring blows of the sword and with words of blood. (*He kills himself and falls. Complete darkness.*)

THE COMMENTATORS: (*Crescendo, as at an auction sale.*) three, five, eight, twelve, eighteen, twenty-five, thirty, thirty-five, forty-eight, fifty-six, eighty, 100, 150, 220, 260, 400, 800, 1700, 2000, 4000, 5000, 12,000, 49,000, 150,000, 220,000, 260,000, 400,000, 800,000, 1,700,000, two million, four million, five million, twelve million, forty-nine million . . .

A: (*Behind the Poet, holding in front of him a screen on which a colored projection falls.*) They put his soul up for auction in Heaven. They buy it by numbers from the cloud of forgetfulness. On the ladder of numbers, they raised the value of his soul. (*He throws the screen over the body of the Poet.*) Everyone is entitled to his own taste. (*The Poet rises to Heaven with the screen.*)

END

(Translated by Aileen Robbins)

Relâche

Francis Picabia

ACT ONE

A white curtain, lowered. A film (to be determined) is shown, lasting about thirty seconds, accompanied by music. [See Picabia notes following scenario.] The curtain rises: the stage is seen to be an oval alcove, completely plastered with white balloons. There is a white carpet. Upstage, a revolving door. The music continues for thirty seconds after the curtain goes up.

A woman gets up from one of the orchestra seats. She is in very elegant evening dress. She climbs onto the stage by means of a practicable.* Music: thirty-five seconds. The moment she appears on stage, the music stops.

The woman stops center stage and examines the set, then stands still. At this moment, the music comes on again for about one minute. When it stops, the woman begins to dance. Choreography to be determined. The music comes on again for a minute and a half; the woman moves upstage and turns three times through the revolving door, then stops, facing the audience.

During this time, thirty men in black suits, white ties, white gloves and opera hats, get up one by one from their seats in the audience, and then climb on stage one after the other, via the practicable. Duration of the music: a minute and a half.

The music stops at the moment when, in a dance to be determined, they surround the woman who has come back to center stage; they circle around her while she disrobes down to pink silk tights, skin tight. Music for forty seconds. The men disperse, and place themselves around the set; the woman stands still for several seconds, while the music comes on again for thirty-five seconds. A few balloons burst in the background.

Everyone dances. The woman is carried off into the wings.

Curtain

---

*A small ramp leading from the orchestra to the stage.

NO INTERMISSION, properly speaking; the music lasts for five minutes with a film of authors sitting down across from one another, having a conversation the text of which is then shown on the screen for ten minutes. No music during the projection of the text.

ACT TWO

The curtain rises. Music for one minute. Electric signs are placed on a black background and alternately flash the names of Erik Satie, Francis Picabia, and Blaise Cendars in different colors.

Two or three powerful stage lights, very powerful, are pointed from the stage out into the theatre. They light the audience, and by shining through disks with holes cut in them, produce a black and white effect. The men enter one by one and encircle the woman's clothes, placed on the floor center stage. Music for twenty seconds.

The woman comes out of the wings, still wearing tights. She wears a crown of orange blossoms on her head: she gets dressed while the men now disrobe, and appears in white silk tights. Music for twenty seconds. A dance, to be determined.

One by one the men regain their seats, where they have left their overcoats. Music for thirty seconds. The woman, left alone on stage, takes a wheelbarrow, piles into it the clothes left by the men, and dumps them in a heap in a corner. Then, moving as close to the front edge of the stage as possible, she takes off her bridal crown and tosses it to one of her dancers, who then places it on the head of a woman planted in the audience.

Music: fifteen seconds.

Then the woman goes back to her seat, as well; the white curtain is lowered, in front of which a small woman appears who dances and sings a song.

Music: forty-five seconds.

The End

(Translated by Jeff Casper)

Francis Picabia's Original Notes for *Entr'Acte*

Wednesday evening.
My dear friend, I am enclosing the ideas for the cinematic part of the ballet.

Yours sincerely,
Francis Picabia

Curtain raiser:
Slow-motion loading of a cannon by Satie and Picabia; the shot must make as much noise as possible. Total length: one minute.
During the interval:
1. Boxing attack by white gloves, on a black screen. Length: fifteen seconds. Written explanatory titles: ten seconds.
2. Game of chess between Duchamp and Man Ray. Jet of water handled by Picabia sweeping away the game: Length: thirty seconds.
3. Juggler and father Lacolique. Length: thirty seconds.
4. Huntsman firing at an ostrich egg on a fountain; a dove comes out of the egg and lands on the huntsman's head; a second huntsman, firing at it, kills the first huntsman: he falls, the bird flies away. Length: one minute. Written titles: twenty seconds.
5. Twenty-one people lying on their backs, showing the soles of their feet. Ten seconds. Handwritten titles: fifteen seconds.
6. Dancer on a transparent mirror, filmed from beneath. Length: one minute. Written titles: five seconds.
7. Blowing-up of rubber balloons and screens, on which figures will be drawn, accompanied by inscriptions. Length: thirty-five seconds.
8. A funeral: hearse drawn by a camel, etc. Length: six minutes. Written titles: one minute.

SELECTED BIBLIOGRAPHY

Appignanesi, Lisa. *The Cabaret*. New York: Universe Books, 1976.

Ashbery, John. "Re-establishing Raymond Roussel." *Portfolio*, No. 6, Autumn 1962, pp. 88-109.

Ball, Hugo. *Flight Out of Time: A Dada Diary*, ed. John Elderfield. New York: Viking, 1974.

Bizarre No. 34-35, Paris, 1964. (Special issue on Roussel.)

Cherniack-Tzuriel, Abba. "Roussel's *Impressions of Africa, The Drama Review*, Vol. 20, No. 2 (T70), June 1976, pp. 108-123.

Dada in Zurich Catalogue. Zurich: Kunsthaus, 1985.

Dada Zeitschriften reprint. Hamburg: Lutz Schulenburg: 1984.

Elderfield, John. *Kurt Schwitters*. New York and London: Thames and Hudson, 1985.

Foster, Stephen (ed.). *dada/dimensions*. Ann Arbor: UMI Research Press, 1985.

Gordon, Mel. "Dada Berlin Performance." *The Drama Review*, Vol. 18, No. 2 (T62), June 1974, pp. 114-133.

Hausmann, Raoul. *Am Anfang War Dada*. Wissmar: Anabas-Verlag, 1970.

Huelsenbeck, Richard. *Memoirs of a Dada Drummer*, ed. Hans J. Kleinschmidt. New York: Viking, 1974.

Lippard, Lucy (ed.). *Dadas on Art*. Englewood Cliffs: Prentice-Hall, Inc., 1971.

Melzer, Annabelle Henkin. *Latest Rage the Big Drum*. Ann Arbor: UMI Research Press, 1980.

Motherwell, Robert (ed.). *Dada Painters and Poets*. New York: Wittenborn, 1951.

Nes Kirby, Victoria. "Georges Ribemont Dessaignes." *The Drama Review*, Vol. 16, No. 1 (T53), March 1972, pp. 104-109.

Ostwald, Hans. *Sittengeschichte der Inflation*. Berlin: Neufeld and Henius, 1931.

Richter, Hans. *Dada: Art and Anti-Art*. New York: Oxford University Press, 1965.

Steinitz, Kate. *Kurt Schwitters: A Portrait from Life*. Berkeley and Los Angeles: University of California, 1968.

Tzara, Tristan. *Seven Dada Manifestos and Lampisteries. Tr. by Barbara Wright. New York: Riverrun Press, 1981.*